CONTENTS

INTRODUCTION

Great job! If you are reading this book, then you have taken the first necessary step toward following one of your dreams: opening a food truck. Food trucks have the potential to be profitable ventures, and many choose to open food trucks because they have lower startup costs, require less business knowledge than other ventures, and because they are a great way to break into the culinary industry. The foodtruckempire.com ran their own survey on 300 food truck business owners and found that 34% of the respondents get between $100,000 and $149,999 as their annual gross income. 21% of the respondents get over $200,000 in annual gross income. 30% of them are in the $150,000 to $200,000 annual gross income bracket.

The best thing about owning a food truck business is that it offers you the freedom of working for yourself. It also offers you the freedom to travel as you take your food truck to different venues. Even other business owners can't boast of this aspect of their business.

This book hopes to provide you with the necessary information to begin your journey towards owning a food truck. Early on, I will go over potential funding sources, how to pick a location, expanding your business, and even details about branding, identity, menu pricing, and even details about expanding your business. By the end of the book, you should have a greater understanding of what it takes to open a food truck business.

While I will provide you with a plan of action and helpful advice, it is up to you to ask yourself why you want to open a food truck, and what kind of food you hope to sell. This book will not focus on the culinary aspect, but instead give advice about the business and marketing of your food truck. Shall we dive in?

**Get Your $397 Bonuses With This Link- https:// bit.ly/2IlMu6l**

- Tax And Accounting Templates**($17 Value)**
- Bookkeeping Basics Tutorial Video**($47 Value)**

- Video Reveals  How To Save Hundreds Of Dollars With A Tax Firm (**$63 Value)**
- Updates When New Food Truck Strategies Are Discovered!**($200 Value)**

# HOW TO STAND OUT FROM THE CROWD

*M*aking your food truck stand out will be essential to your success. For those prospective food truck owners based in large cities with a wide selection of food trucks, you will want to pay close attention to this chapter. In this part of the book, I will be going over all the ways you can bring positive attention to your food truck, how to form a brand and identity for your food truck, and share a story of one food truck owner's experience in forming an identity for his business. Customers are hit with options every day, so it is important that you form a brand and identity that will help your food truck business bring in customers.

## What Is a Food Truck Brand?

To put this simply, a food truck brand is simply the combination of all of the emotions, images, and ideas that come to mind when people think of your food truck. It could be that a customer pictures your truck right away, think of your funny menu titles, or even perhaps the logo. Your brand is everything that is memorable with your business. Create a brand for your food truck that is so distinct that when someone hears your truck's name, they instantly imagine its image, brand, and the taste of your food. Making a quality brand for your food truck gives your customers the opportunity to develop a connection to your food truck and your food, and it is your responsibility to define that connection and develop it. You are in charge of forming the images you want people to associate with your food truck and your name. Many food truck businesses focus on one concept they want people to imagine; therefore, a good exercise to start building your brand is to think of one word that you want people to associate your food truck with the most. For some people, this might be "sweet;" for others it could be "cowboy" or "wholesome." Once you have that one word in mind, you can begin to build your brand from there.

A great place to find creative people to develop unique logos, signs, menu and other branding material for your food truck is on a site like Fiverr. This is a platform for freelance services which connects businesses with freelancers that need their services world wide. You can find graphic designers with extraordinary ideas to bring your dream to life.

### Cultivating That One Word

Once you have that one word in mind, you need to find ways to exude the energy of that word. If you picked "cowboy" for example, and you sell quality BBQ meals, how else might you give off that same energy? For some food trucks, this will come down to how they dress—maybe you want to have uniforms for your staff that stand out. Other people might focus on their online presence or how they speak to customers. Start writing a list of some simple things you can do to exude the essence of your word.

Your brand will be that *guarantee* you make to your customers. It is about the kind of experience you plan to offer and who your truck is. This should not be confused with other forms of marketing, like ads; advertisements are all about bringing in new customers at the door, whereas your brand is about making yourself known and recognizable and translating who you are as a business. Food truck businesses, more than others, need to focus on their brand over their advertising. People who visit food trucks are often looking for a specific experience and food. You will want to show how you can give a unique experience to your customers with your brand. One way to give people a push to try your food truck is by creating an inviting and catchy logo and catchphrase that can grab their attention. Catchphrases cause many people to stumble with their brand identity, but they're not too hard to develop when you start by building off the one word you selected earlier. For example, if your word was "sweet" and you sell cupcakes, perhaps your catch phrase could be something like "Daisy's Desserts: We're the cherry on top of your day." From there, you can even choose to add a signature cherry on top of all of your desserts. Maybe you make customer stamp cards with cherry stamps. While the word "sweet" wasn't technically in the catchphrase, the essence of "sweet" was built in with a kind and simple phrase, the name daisy, and cherries.

### THREE THINGS That Will Make Your Brand Effective

All great brands have three key features that can make them more effective. We will take a look at each one.

1. **Great brands are easy to recognize**. Think of all the food trucks you have gone to and which have been your favorite. When you went to order food, did you recognize it from down the street? Can you picture it clearly in your mind? People should be

able to imagine your food truck easily once they hear your name. Therefore, be sure to focus extensively on the design aspect of your brand—there are some food trucks that have become memorable on food network shows strictly because of their identity. One in particular comes to mind: a three-women food truck team that sold hotdogs, but their brand was all about patriotism. They wore American flag attire, sold classic American foods, and had a truck with a simple yet patriotic logo. Decide what you are willing to do to make your food truck stand out and do that. If that involves a costume, then don't be afraid to dress up!

2. **Create a clear emotional appeal**. All memorable brands have some kind of evident emotional appeal, and it should not just be an association with hunger; people should want to go to your food truck for the feeling they get from being there. If you are "Daisy's desserts," maybe a customer goes there because they want to have a kind interaction and enjoy a relaxing moment with some dessert. Some food trucks focus on creating an energy of "excess," "fun," or "wacky." What is the emotion you want people to associate with your food truck? Ask yourself that, then try to find ways you can offer that emotion to your customers.

3. **Make sure you are consistent**. You should not flip flop your brand. What I mean by this is that you shouldn't try to give a "fun" experience one week,

then opt for a "wholesome" meal the next. Once you make a decision, stick with it. If it really isn't working after six months or a year, that would be when you decide to try and change it. However, try to not make drastic changes while you are in the process of forming your first brand and identity. You want people to expect a certain kind of experience from your food truck, and you want to provide that experience every time.

### What Is a Food Truck Identity? Here Is Why You Need One.

A food truck brand encompasses a great deal of things related to your food truck, but an *identity* is all about the experience and personality you offer your customers. It is your truck's reputation. When your customers think of your food truck, you want them to think of the customer experience, how employees treat the customer, and also your presence on social media. All of these would also end up including your company's values. There are three key things that can help form your brand identity.

1. **How you accurately send your message**. When a person goes to your food truck, in addition to all the branding elements, the way you and your employees interact with your customer should convey a clear message. What do you want to convey and how are

you making it clear? The last thing you want is for your customers to get a sense of "fun" from your brand, then when they place an order or read your social media interactions, they get a pretentious sternness. You need to convey your message accurately through all forms of your identity.

2. **How you implement creativity**. Are you being original in regard to your identity? Is your menu creative? Oftentimes, people become too caught up in being clear or short with their menu, but that is one easy way to add some creative flair. Social media is another way to implement creativity. If you choose to handle your social media accounts, it may be wise to take a small course in marketing and online presence; otherwise, consider hiring a freelancer to handle this aspect of your business a few times a week.

3. **In what ways are you consistent?** I mentioned consistency when it came to your brand, but you also need to be consistent with your identity. Are you doing all you can to show your identity through your message and creativity? Are they both in line with each other? Ask others for their opinions in regard to your identity in brand and share mockups of your design and menu. The best way you can aim for consistency is to do a market test with people you both know and don't know. Your identity and your brand are the two things you can

easily control when you begin your food truck business.

## Here's a Brief Story...

I was consulting with a food truck company recently that had seen a small decrease in customers that used to visit them regularly. They weren't sure what the problem was—the owner was at every shift and he often made it a point to memorize his customers' names and greet them. They cooked southern food, so it was very important to him that his customers felt welcome and "at home." When I began looking into the issue, I was a bit confused at first too. Their identity seemed to be strong, and they had great customer service that was in line with their brand. The menu mimicked the atmosphere, and the design of the truck also matched their southern sweet style. Finally, I asked about social media. It was only when I began looking through all of their accounts that I noticed the real problem: the owner had been managing all the accounts. And while he was big on traditional living, that was not creating the same inviting environment he aimed to create in person. People would ask questions about menu items, weekly specials, and locations through direct messages, and it would sometimes take him full days to respond. Whenever he did respond, he was often exhausted and would respond with little information. What he didn't realize was that people took those quick, few-word responses to be a stark contrast from his in-person friendliness. The slow responses also caused some people not to go because they were unsure about a menu item or location details. We ended up solving the problem by having him take a quick social media lesson from his teenage daughter. She also ended up helping him manage it!

**In Conclusion**

Your brand and your identity are two essential aspects of having a successful food truck business. Once you move through the hurtle of securing funding and preparing your food truck, your branding will be something that will not require a financial investment, but rather, a big time-and-energy investment. I have given you some clear advice to work with—now it is up to you to figure out exactly what message and ideas you want your customers to walk away with, then do your best to recreate that message in every possible way.

## WHAT KIND OF FOOD TRUCK SHOULD I BUY?

One of the most important decisions you will make at the start of your food truck business is deciding which type of food truck you will buy. This is not a quick decision, but with the help of this chapter, I hope to make the decision-making process simpler. I'll go over some of the more popular food trucks, share some of their features, and also make suggestions about which kind of food trucks might do well with this type of truck. What you may or may not know is that there are a variety of "food trucks" available to you, depending on your prep needs. A food truck can be as simple as a heating unit in a pick-up truck, or as complex as a camper turned sit-down restaurant. Hopefully, by the end of this chapter, you will have an idea of which truck is best for you.

. . .

## FOOD CART

A food cart is different than the food truck you might imagine initially, in that it is a small cart towed to a location by another vehicle. Typically, these are a couple hundred square feet and don't have much space, so you will be limited on what you can and cannot do. Often, these do have some sort of power, though not as much as traditional food trucks. Because of their size, they definitely do cost less in terms of operation compared to larger food trucks. You can spend an estimated $3,000 on the cart itself not considering the food and other operational costs. Food carts might be a good idea for someone who plans to have a small-scale business selling food like ice cream or snacks, as they will be fairly easy to operate with only one person. Some limitations obviously include the size, and there are also some issues in terms of location—once you park, you will need to be towed again to move to a new location if the current one turns out to be undesirable. Startup costs for a food cart are significantly lower than a full-scale food truck.

## FOOD TRAILERS

These are similar to food carts, in that they also have to be towed to a location. Unlike food carts, however, they offer ample space and the option for a full-sized kitchen. With the option for a larger kitchen, a food trailer can service many more customers than a food cart. Trailers have an aesthetic that many companies enjoy, and unlike full-service food trucks, they are a more affordable option. They can cost an estimated $50,000 on the cheaper end.

Food trucks can be purchased in a variety of sizes, and the generator is often located outside the truck, leaving much more space inside. The downside of this form of food truck, however, is that most food trailers cannot be parked on the street in the same way that a food truck can be. On the other hand, they can be parked in places that allow stationary trailers. These are a good option for someone who has a few locations set in mind where trailers are allowed, and for someone who needs a good amount of kitchen space. Food trailers also offer a lot of storage. If you have less money to invest and have spaces in mind to park, it might be a good idea to invest in a trailer while you save up for a more portable option.

**Bustaurant**

A bustaurant is just what it sounds like—a bus that holds a mini restaurant inside. In some major cities, people have started creating a new kind of food truck experience by purchasing a double decker bus and converting it into a mini diner. Some people have even gone ahead to convert an RV into a food truck. Others have converted U-Hauls into bustaurants. These also have kitchens built inside, though there are regulations for how the kitchen can be used. To begin, the kitchen cannot be used while the vehicle is in operation. Some bustaurants have fought this regulation by prepping the food while parked and serving while on the move. Other bustaurants opt for only serving food while they are parked. Seating is always an issue when you own a food truck business; although, some owners choose not to consider that a priority, whereas others opt to only park in places that offer seating to their customers. Busteraunts offer an even better solution, which is a chance to dine inside the bus while the food is prepared.

There do exist some disadvantages to choosing this for your food truck business, however. A double decker bus is very expensive and can cost a few $100 thousand. Also, to drive one of these vehicles, you will need to acquire a commercial license. The size may also be a bit of an issue. Some places may be more welcoming to traditional food trucks, though they may not be so welcoming to a double-decker bus. Such vehicles might take up too much space, both vertically and horizontally. Nevertheless, it could still be a good option if you have a cuisine that may benefit from a sit-down experience. It could also be beneficial if you are in a major city that offers places to park and with little food truck competition of the same style.

## Types of Vehicles That Might Make Great Food Trucks

**Nissan Cargo:** This van is a V8, has the potential to two over 8,000 pounds, and has a very high interior roof. There is plenty of storage inside and a rack outside to stack items like chairs or a small table. The Nissan Cargo also has electrical outlets that give as much as 400 watts of power, and there is one in both the front and back of the cabin. For those who need a small area to work inside, this vehicle offers a fold down seat in the front that can be made into a makeshift desk. These vans are also very affordable at only about $30,000 each and an estimated $22,000 for a used car. These vehicles are a great option if the prep work is easy and you require less space than a traditional food truck.

Ford Transit Full Size: These vans offer three different lengths and heights for its room. It also comes with two options for the wheelbases. In general, Ford Transit Full Sizes are spacious vehicles and can easily house a cook who is over six feet tall without having them have to hunch. There is enough space inside for a variety of equipment, which also makes them capable of being used by food truck owners who plan to do a lot of cooking on site. They can be purchased for between $30,000 and $45,000 for a used and new vehicle.

FREIGHTLINER SPRINTER CREW VAN: This high-ceilinged van offers large windows that allow plenty of light to enter inside. They can have AC and heat in the cooking area if needed, along with a plethora of other upgrading options. These vehicles have the potential to tow over 7,000 pounds, making them ideal for any food truck business that needs to tow barbecue grills or smokers. These can be purchased for around $50,000 with many of the mentioned features. New food truck owners often choose this option because of its customization potential. There are so many features (like an extra battery) that can be added, making it easily into a food truck that can fit your needs. An used freightliner sprinter crew van would cost around $33,000.

FORD CUTAWAY: Yes, that is right—your basic ambulance vehicle can also be turned into a food truck and bought for a great price. In used condition, they run for about $20,000, making them a great option for new food truck businesses. They are also customizable. Because of how these emergency vehicles are usually used, they come with plenty of storage already installed making them easy to turn into full scale food trucks. They can be outfitted with extra batteries, air conditioning, and even lockable storage space outside the truck. Because these have been used to transport injured people and bodies, it is something to consider before purchasing. Are you able to tolerate that knowledge? If so, they are a wonderful option for first-time food truck businesses because of their affordability and how easily they can be customized.

Health inspectors will not need you to offer any additional paperwork as long as the ambulance adheres to the guidelines for a food truck.

VOLKSWAGEN WESTFALIA BUS: If you are looking for affordable options, this one might be the vehicle for you. The Westfalia Pop Up bus has many features that can make them a great option for starter food truck owners. Used, they can be bought for under $16,000. They are surprisingly roomy with plenty of space to set up a functioning kitchen. Because they have a pop-up top, they are a great option to have if you want to set up a seating area or a small desk for cash handling. Many later models also include things like a sink, spacious storage, and some towing capabilities. For those who do not plan on having complex menus and want to get started with very little startup, these might be a great option for you. They are also much easier to drive because of their size and will make finding a parking spot easier than it would be for larger trucks.

CITROËN H VAN: This is a great option to combine with the purchase of a food trailer. They have the power to tow a large trailer, while the inside is big enough to manage the same operating capabilities as a small food truck. Many people choose these vehicles when starting a food truck for coffee or desserts, as both require minimal prep space. If you want the option for both a trailer and smaller scale food truck, this might be your best bet. If your menu involves more prep and less cooking time, you could prepare food, load it in the van, and sell from this vehicle. For larger events, you can take the full-size trailer and sell your main menu items. For anyone looking to start a small food truck business that primarily sells easy-to-make or premade goods, this is a great van for a good price.

DIY: If you have the finances and time, you might want to choose to build your own food truck. The nice thing about choosing to build your own food truck is that you can work within your own budget and with just about any vehicle you choose. If you are able to get a great deal on a used van or truck that you think could easily fit your food truck needs, you should consider this route. Though it might take some time to create the food truck you want, you can end up saving a lot of money versus going the route of customizing a food truck brand new. In addition, you could opt for equipment financing, versus other higher interest loans.

**Buy new and customized:** There are many food truck companies that will design a food truck with your specific needs in mind. If you can get a high amount of financing and are okay with spending more upfront, you might want to think about investing in a custom food truck. There are many advantages to doing this. To begin, you will be able to set it up exactly how you'd like it for your business. Most of the time, these come with a warranty that will come in handy should any issues arise within the food truck. In addition to customizing the interior, you can often have the exterior customized as part of the purchasing price. If you opt to do this, be sure you find a reputable maker who has created successful food trucks for other companies that have lasted for many years. A new, customized truck will cost over $50,000.

## In Conclusion

There are numerous food truck options available to you, and this chapter aimed to offer you selections within a wide budget range. As you prepare to purchase your food truck, make sure you have a clear idea of what you will be cooking or selling. If your menu is mainly off site prep, premade, dessert, or beverage-focused, you may not need a brand new, heavily upgraded, food truck, even if you have the budget for it. The best way to give your profits a boost early is by saving your money when you purchase your food truck. Go with what will be the absolute best for your business; not necessarily the best available model or largest size.

## How to Hone in on Your Customer

In the previous chapter, I went over the importance of creating a brand and identity for your food truck. But, did you know it is also important that you create your "ideal customer?" If running a business is a new venture for you, you may be thinking *well any customer is my ideal customer*, but that should never be the case. Although you can be grateful for all business that comes your way, it is absolutely essential that you have an ideal demographic, as it will help your business stay afloat and succeed. This will also help you see when you are being successful and when you might need to rethink some aspects of your business. The best food trucks know their market and how to sell to them. A BBQ meat specialty food truck will not aim to sell to vegans, for example; they may have some vegan options, but ultimately, their goal is to make their meat enthusiast customers happy. Thus, you too need to figure out exactly who your ideal customer is.

## Define Your Ideal Customer

To identify your key demographics, I want you to play the role of a writer for now and create your ideal customer as a character. Here are some questions you will need to ask yourself:

· **What is the age range of your ideal customer?** *(Go for a 10 to 15-year range)*

o Finding out the age range of your customer will assist you in knowing what kind of marketing angle to take. Younger customers will likely require heavy social media marketing, along with special kinds of promotions. Older customers might do better with a different type of marketing, such as direct mail, coupon marketing, or a specific shift.

· **What gender is your ideal customer?**

o The gender of your ideal customer might be tied more directly to the customer interests which we will discuss later on. If you have an ideal gender in mind, then you can decide how to best approach your design and branding.

· **What is their income level?**

o This question will help you decide how much to charge for your food, along with what kind of meals might do well. If you have an ideal customer who is willing to splurge on meals, you can probably work with more premium ingredients; however, if your customer has a lower income, you will likely want to offer more specials and work with affordable ingredients that allow you to have a lower selling cost.

· **What is the education status of your ideal customer?**

o This consideration will look into the influence of the language you use when marketing, how you organize your menu, where you decide to locate your truck, and also potential interests of your customers.

· **Does your ideal customer work? What kind of careers might they have?**

o People with certain careers have different meal needs than people in other career paths. Nurses, for example, work very long shifts and likely eat out more during work hours than off hours.

· **Is your ideal customer married? Single? A casual dater?**

o Their marital status would influence their interests, how many meals they eat out, along with where they might frequent. Knowing this information can help you make choices that will lead to higher sales.

· **What is the size of your ideal customer's household?**

o Do you want to sell to customers who go out as a family of four, for example? When you see your ideal customer coming up to your window, do you normally envision a couple, single person, or family? Knowing this will help you organize your menu, specials, and pricing better.

· **Does your ideal customer have a religion they follow?**

o Some religions have certain food restrictions— is this important to you? Do you plan on changing your menu for them? Some religions hold certain values, so you should be wondering whether your company values some ideals more than others.

ONCE YOU HAVE a specific customer in mind, it will make your business choices much easier. Instead of having to make choices you think will make the most money, you can focus on choices that will appease your ideal customer the most. For example, instead of finding all the best locations in your city, you would only need to find the best locations for your customer's demographics.

I'll give you an example—a homestyle cooking truck's main demographic might be a man in his mid-forties who is looking for a meal that reminds him of his mother's food after a long day of construction work. He would make about $55 thousand a year. Would this food truck be successful parking in the busiest part of Mission Beach, California? This city is an absolute tourist hub and is filled with college students; therefore, no, this would not be their ideal location. Now, would the same truck do well if they park in San Diego, California, near a large construction zone and during lunch hour or near sundown? They are likely to do much better in the second location because they have placed themselves where their ideal customers are. This is how narrowing down your market can ensure you make the right choices for your business.

### Defining Your Target Market

It is not enough to simply *know* your ideal demographic however; now you need to find out more about them. The information I gave you above about the man were details I assumed, but you can find out information of your demographic through research. Find out what interests they have, their lifestyle, and learn more about what they find valuable in businesses. We can gather from the above information that the customer probably values a quality price and a relatively quick speed. Why can we assume this? His income is not substantial, and he enjoys buying food after work on his way out, so he's probably exhausted from his physical job. Some demographics are more concerned with sustainability than others, whereas some demographics are willing to pay more for food that has been handled a certain way. When you define your target market, you will know how to reach them better.

### WHERE IS YOUR TARGET MARKET?

In an earlier chapter, we discussed finding the best locations; however, even the most populated areas won't be helpful if your food truck is not a good fit for that area. Once you define your ideal customer and their interests, it is important that you take the time to find out where you can locate those customers. If you live in a major metropolitan area, you would likely have a couple places that are each known as the "downtown," "arts district," or "business district." You will want to find out where in your city your ideal customer goes most often. One way to do this would be to look up businesses that likely have a similar customer demographic to you. If you have a vegan food truck, find local vegan restaurants that seem to be consistently busy. Where are these located within the city? What do they do to attract their ideal customers?

Another easy way to learn about demographic details is by visiting the US Census Bureau website. If you go to their website, you can search up a local zip code and find out the key demographics of people living in that area. With this information, you can learn what local zip codes in which it might be best for you to sell your food.

## OTHER WAYS You Can Learn More About Your Demographic and Market

Small Business Development Centers (SBDC) can often be found on college campuses, or you can also browse the Association of Small Business Development Centers (ASBDC) to find your local SBDC. These centers are for the community and are nonprofit, thus making them a great resource for finding information. You can reach out to them to learn more about marketing, financial issues, organizing, and even producing.

You might also want to look into research companies. Some companies provide demographic information easily on the internet, though usually require a large fee (a few hundred to $3,000) for the information. From that information, however, you will learn about your market demographics and information on economic development, and you can have the information specific to your location. Research firms also offer focus group opportunities. These vary in cost and also depend on what you are willing to pay; however, a focus group will give you the chance to hear firsthand what customers think about your food. You can make the focus group specific to the demographics you are hoping to reach, food tasting, or you could also ask about branding, design, advertising, among other subjects.

During a focus group, the research firm will ask questions to help you learn how relevant the answers are. They might ask about the participants' knowledge of food trucks, how much they are willing to pay for a certain food item, or even how much they know about a specific type of cuisine. The research firm does the entire job of locating participants, organizing the panel, and paying them, which is why they often have a fairly large fee. However, it is a great opportunity to learn more about your key demographics more honestly. In comparison, you would learn more from a focus group than you will by asking your friends to participate in the same process.

**In Conclusion**

It is not enough to simply say "every customer is my ideal customer." You need to know exactly who you are trying to reach; otherwise, every decision you make will become a guessing game and decision based on chance. Knowing your ideal customer will influence your menu, costs, location choices, and branding.

# HOW TO FIND THE BEST LOCATION

Once you have figured out how to make a profit
through your menu costs, it is time to move on to
another big aspect of owning a food truck: your
location. Deciding where you want to park your
food truck may seem like an easy feat at first, but
there are a lot of things you need to consider. This
chapter will guide you through some of the legal
aspects of deciding where to park your food truck,
while also giving you helpful tips on securing prime
locations for your truck. Unlike a brick and mortar
restaurant, you do have some flexibility, which can
mean that if you don't do well in one location, you
can decide to venture out and try a new location the
next day. In fact, you have a higher chance of making
more money if you try out new places frequently.

Deciding where to park can either lead to great
profits or excess work for little pay. Also food trucks

can run throughout the year as long as you tweak your menu to the weather. The following are some guidelines and suggestions to follow when looking for where to park your food truck.

## COMMON FOOD TRUCK **Parking Areas**

This list is a good starting point for finding where to park your food truck. Often, these areas will have looser requirements when it comes to zoning and city laws. They will also likely be more welcoming to your presence. These places will often have enough space and enough customers to help boost your sales.

## Farmers Markets

Farmers markets can be a great option, given their frequent meetings and high amounts of foot traffic. Most cities have a farmers market that meets monthly, whereas some larger cities might have multiple farmers markets that meet weekly or throughout the month. Whether a farmers market is a good choice for you will likely depend on the menu. We will be talking about customers later in the book, but for now, it might be a good idea to think about who will be most likely to buy your food. If you are a vegan-focused or a farm-to-table style food truck, you may do very well at a farmers market in which people enjoy shopping for fresh produce. On the other hand, if your food truck contains more carnival-style foods, you may not do as well here. That does not technically mean you shouldn't try at all, but you should simply consider how you price your food and what you should focus on selling at the farmers market. These locations are great if you have seasonal menu items, and you should even consider partnering with another vendor and featuring their items (local honey, for example) in one of your menu items.

**Festivals**

Festivals are fun events that people attend to hear live music, watch artists, dance, and enjoy meeting like-minded people. These events generally last many hours for a few days in a row, so they are filled with people in search of multiple meals a day. Typically, festivals have thousands of attendees; therefore, there will be ample space for food trucks and foot traffic. Festivals, like farmers markets, will also have their specific needs. There are usually a lot of food trucks at these types of events, so you will want to keep your menu simple and easy to carry. Most people at festivals are moving from one space to the next or buying food and eating it elsewhere, so certain menu items are likely to do better than others (burritos, sandwiches, and tacos are easy to carry around the festival, whereas soup or pasta will be more difficult and less appealing). These events are usually only held once a year, so if the event is profitable for you, it is important you stay in touch and attend again the following year. Some festivals can help boost your profits in the span of only a few days because of how much traffic is built into the event. However, be prepared for long hours and a high quantity of orders.

## FOOD TRUCK PARKS

Food trucks have become so popular in recent years that there are now "food truck parks," which are typically empty lots with picnic tables set up. At certain times of the week, multiple food trucks can drive over and park for a set number of hours. These locations are built for food trucks; therefore, their requirements are likely not as strict. In addition, people who visit food truck parks are often interested in trying out multiple dishes from multiple parks, which means food truck parks are great for networking with other owners as well. Now, while networking is great, it does come with one clear disadvantage—competition. Oftentimes, you may come face-to-face with your truck's major competitor. The key to doing well at food truck parks is to make a menu that features small, à la carte items.

Work with the idea that people want to try multiple kinds of foods and focus on smaller portions and variety. If you can put together a sample platter, you are more likely to succeed. If you decide to join a weekly food truck park meetup, don't let the competition discourage you; this type of location is likely to vary weekly in profit influx.

## Business Districts

Depending on the city you are operating in, it will likely have a major business district. A business district is a set few blocks where multiple businesses are located. These are typically large, high-rise buildings with hundreds of employees who work nine to five jobs. Business districts are a great option for parking your food truck, especially during the week and during lunch hour. Some business districts have specific days when they would allow food trucks to come by and, most of the time, their employees know this fact ahead of time. This means you will likely have hundreds of employees who have planned to eat out for that day. The key to succeeding in these locations is time management; you will want to plan meals that are quick and easy to prepare. Many employees will be on 30-minute or one-hour lunch breaks, which they won't want to spend waiting in line for food. So, think about the type of specials you can offer to these employees—

are there special wraps you can make? Easy-to-prep salads? You will want to stay away from any foods that take a while to prepare. If customers find your truck takes longer than others nearby, they will be less likely to go to yours, even if they prefer your food, because of time limitations.

### BARS OR CLUBS

These are especially profitable if you live in an area that has a very active nightlife. Bars and night-clubs do not typically sell food, but they do sell plenty of alcohol. As you may know, when people drink and dance for hours, they would usually find themselves in need of a midnight snack at closing time. If you can find a popular nightclub or bar in your area, and you can set up at a park nearby, you will probably catch some people as they exit the bar.

Food trucks are not allowed to sell alcohol generally to the public. But under certain circum-stances they can sell alcoholic beverages as long as they are in private events and have the correct permits allowing them to serve alcohol. Some of the permits needed for the food truck to sell alcohol include the alcohol catering license and the special events permits. New Orleans allows alcohol selling to the public but only in the quarter. But in other states if you do not have these and are not in an event you are not going to be able to sell alcohol. So on a regular day parking near a club or bar is your best option.

Drunk customers are often willing to pay a little bit more for quality food in the late midnight hours, especially if nearby restaurants are closed. These types of venues will be especially profitable for you if you sell foods that pair well with alcohol—think non-farmer market menus. Items like french fries, tater tots, pizza, sandwiches, burritos, and tacos will likely do very well during midnight hours. It might also be a good idea to introduce yourself to the owner of the bar or nightclub and let them know you are interested in parking nearby. If you can get on good terms with them, they may even want to help you avoid some legal aspects of zoning by letting you park close by and using their resources.

## Surprisingly, Gas Stations

The key to finding a good gas station in which to park is to look for one that is larger and more commercial. In this case, you might want to search for one close to major freeways. Oftentimes, people will be looking for a snack or meal on their way home, and if you can offer food that is better than the pizza slices that have been sitting out for hours, customers may be more inclined to pay a higher cost for the food you are offering, merely so they can have food of slightly higher quality. Many gas station owners appreciate having food trucks park nearby, as it catches the attention of customers who are also likely to fill up on gas while stopping by your food truck. The key with gas stations, however, is to get approval before you show up. Introduce yourself to the owner and ask if you can sell from that location; they will most often be accepting of your proposal. These venues are a great place to sell food that can be easily wrapped to go, snacked on while driving, or will stay warm until the driver makes it home.

## Street Parking

This may seem like a logical choice, but sometimes, people have a hard time figuring out how it works, or they are somewhere they don't want to deal with. Street parking your food truck is a great way to bring in customers, but you do need to be particular about where you park. To begin, you should consider the type of customers you want to service (which we will discuss in more detail in a later chapter). If your food truck specializes in ice cream desserts, you will want to focus your street parking efforts on hot days and in areas where there will probably be more people who would want an icy treat. On colder days you could sell hot chocolate or christmas cookies during the christmas festivities. This setting could be a park, skating rink, skateboarding park, or near a beach, depending on where you live and where the Christmas shopping traffic is highest. If your truck, however, sells upscale salad entrées, you may want to focus your efforts on finding street parking near businesses or in areas where there are people looking for a fulfilling and wholesome meal. Street parking is also possible near major shopping centers or malls. If you live in a major city, street parking could be a great option for your food truck.

## Near Colleges and Universities

There are actually many universities that have "Food Truck Tuesdays" or "Farmers Markets," for which food trucks can get a contract and show up at once a week or once a month. College students typically don't have the resources to cook for themselves, and while they may have meals on campus, they are—or will be—probably tired of the same options every day. Students are often willing to spend money to experience new and unique food. If you can't get a contract at a park within the university, you might be able to secure a street parking spot near a university park close to a college. If you can do this, you can use your social media or even hand out fliers to let people know where you will be each week. Even though there are plenty of restaurants near college campuses, college students are likely to venture out to a food truck if it means trying a new food item. If you can get a permit (which may cost between $100 and $500), or permission, it might be a good idea to show up during lunch hours or major sporting events. It's definitely worth a try if you sell unique food that is unlike other offerings in the area.

The Best Cities to Run a Food Truck Business

The best cities that are favorable to a food truck business include Philadelphia which has over 100 food trucks operating in the city. Cleveland is another food truck friendly city with over 40 food trucks operating. Also consider cities like San Francisco, Atlanta,Houston, Portland and Vancouver. These are places where this type of businesses have thrived for years opening the food industry to more opportunities.

## Laws to Keep in Mind

It is important, once you start your food truck business, that you take the time to research your state laws. Some cities and states have specific laws on where food trucks can be parked; for example, in one state, food trucks cannot be parked within 30 feet of a brick and mortar restaurant. Some states may require you request a permit before parking at a community park, whereas some may have rules about parking near schools. It is a good idea to research this before you begin selling in your city.

If you plan on parking somewhere for the long term, and it is near a major business with thousands of employees, it might be a good idea to create a revocable license agreement, which can be cancelled or revoked at any time. You can set these contracts up so that both you and the business know where you can or cannot park, and you will know what you are held accountable for in regard to customers and cleanliness. If you are trying to secure a spot on a college campus, you will need to get a permit; however, they are very easy to obtain from the administration.

Wherever you decide to park, you will need to take some time to research your specific city and state laws. Some places have stricter requirements than others, and it may be a good idea to focus your efforts on research before you get out to make your first sales. A food truck park or a farmers market will probably be the easiest places to begin.

**In Conclusion**

Food trucks offer the benefit of change. With a food truck, you can alter where you visit and park whenever you want, but it is a good idea to find some areas where you plan to park frequently. A farmers market is a great place to begin, as you would typically have to check in with the farmers market administration before parking, versus checking in with your local city legislation. It's a good idea to drive around in your spare time (though not in your food truck) to search for any potential hotspots for customers. Consider trying out a new type of venue each week. It is also necessary that you develop good marketing strategies, as many of your return customers will probably be trying to find your location through social media. We will be talking about that in more depth in a later chapter.

## How to Price Your Food and Menu

Now that you have an idea of how you can plan to finance your food truck, it is time to work out the details of profit. Your profit will come from the food you sell more than anything else (drinks, tips, etc.), but that does not mean you should continue raising your food costs, for a higher immediate profit. Figuring out how much for which to sell your menu items is a tricky game. You will want to make sure your costs are high enough that you are making a reasonable profit after the labor and ingredient costs, but not so high that you drive away your customers. Customers can be quite particular about food costs—if they suspect they are being over-charged, they will likely travel elsewhere for the same product. This is especially true for food trucks where the food is the reason they buy, as opposed to the service or atmosphere of a full-scale restaurant. This chapter will help make menu pricing easier by guiding you through the process in easy-to-follow steps.

## Two Big Pricing Mistakes to Avoid

Before we begin going through the steps, I want to go over some simple mistakes that you must avoid as a new food truck operator. The following are common pitfalls people fall into when pricing out their menus as new food truck owners:

1. **Pricing items based on cost alone**. This is an easy to make mistake—people think they can keep costs relatively low by pricing out items based on the cost of production. Many new food truck owners take the cost of production and add a small markup, which is a terrible mistake, as doing so does not account for labor or whether the customer is willing to pay for that item. While it is important to know how much it costs to make a menu item, it does not mean that cost needs to be the majority of the price itself when selling it to the customer.

2. **Pricing based on competitor pricing**. I know I said that cost was a big reason a customer may or

may not go to your food truck, but basing your prices purely on the prices your competitors have set is another terrible idea. Many new food truck owners aim to create a price point that is somewhere in the middle of the highest and lowest local competitor costs, but doing so leaves out so many variables. For starters, it does not take into account the cost of production at all, meaning that there may be moments when you are losing money on a menu item because you chose to price a certain way. Likewise, a competitor may have certain vendor costs and privileges that you don't have, which would allow them to price an item a certain way. In short, this is not a pricing method that is sustainable in the long term, and it could lead to potential profit and/or customer loss.

## Calculating Your Menu Costs

### Step One: Know your Direct and Indirect Costs

Now that I have shown you some clear mistakes you should avoid when pricing out your menu items, I will be sharing the best way to price your menu items so you can maximize your profit and increase customer retention. To begin, we will be going over two important factors that you will need to know when pricing out your menu: direct costs and indirect costs. It is important that you under-stand these costs, not only for your menu pricing, but also for your general business accounting as well.

Direct costs are the immediate costs associated with each food item, which would include the cost of every single ingredient—even that tablespoon of oil you use to sauté food. It also includes food that is thrown away during cooking (bay leaves, if some-thing is caked in salt, etc.). You should be calculating direct costs at *cost per serving*. Indirect costs are the costs associated with preparing the food. This can include serving items, cost to operate the oven or fryer, etc.

Once you know these two types of costs and the differences between them, you can use them to help influence the pricing of your menu items. They should not be used alone to figure out the cost, but rather in combination with the steps I provide to you.

### STEP TWO: Decide on Your Added Value and Add It to Your Direct and Indirect Costs

Chances are, if you are building a food truck business, you are doing it to offer a brand new food to the community. Most food trucks find their appeal from their originality. Are you adding a spin on a traditional cuisine? Are you selling fusion food?

Are you offering food for a certain lifestyle that isn't found easily? Whatever the case, the unique aspect of your business will also be something that adds value to your food. If, for example, you are the only vegan food truck and the only one to sell specialty sandwiches, it would mean that you have a hard-to-find offering—in turn, adding value to your food. This added value can be included as part of your total prep cost (direct, indirect, and added value costs). Aside from unique value, there are other ways you can add value costs to your food items. Do you use organic or free-range ingredients? Either of these would automatically boost your meals to a higher standard. If you are allergy-friendly (celiac-friendly or nut allergy-friendly), you can also add this to your value cost. Along with these considerations, freshness and portion sizes can all also increase the value of your unique food.

### Step Three: Decide on Your Markup

Most restaurants and food truck businesses create their menu item costs by taking the total prep cost (indirect, direct, and added value) and dividing it by a percentage ranging from 20% to 40% more than the total direct and indirect costs. This means that if you have a taco that cost you $1, you should make your cost range between $2.50 to $5. How much or how little by which you decide to divide will be based on your added value. If you are the only vegan taco truck around and you use premium ingredients, it might be a better idea to have a higher markup. The higher the percentage, the lower your overall cost will be; likewise, the higher you go in percentage, the more items you have to sell to increase your profits. If your $1 taco, for example, is easy-to-find and comes in a small serving size, you might be more confident in selling many tacos for $2.50 instead of trying to sell fewer tacos for $5. The important thing to remember here is that you make your costs reasonable. No one will pay $5 for a street taco-sized carne asada taco, especially if your food truck is based in San Diego. However, they will be more likely to pay $5 for a larger taco that is made to taste like carnitas when it is really jackfruit, especially if you go to an area where vegan options are harder to find.

In addition to the method mentioned above, another common strategy for pricing is the 1/3 method. This strategy basically takes the total indirect and direct costs and considers that to be 1/3 of the customer price. This leaves 2/3 of the selling price as part of the profit and operation costs. Based on this method, your $1 taco should sell for $3. It does not take into account much of the "added value;" thus, this might be a better option for someone who is offering food items that are not necessarily unique, but still valued.

Take, for example, a traditional taco truck or a hot dog and hamburger food truck. Whichever option you use, you'll need to keep in mind this keyword: *balance*. However much you choose to mark up your cost will be essentially how much profit you will make on an item, but don't mark up your prices so high that you lose your customers.

### OTHER THINGS TO Keep in Mind When Pricing

I've now given you a handy three-step system to pricing your food items, but there are still other things that might influence your prices. You should also remember that prices are not meant to be set in stone; they should fluctuate periodically, even if only for occasional sales.

· LABOR COSTS: Does your menu require a chef who is specially trained in a certain kind of cuisine? If so, your labor costs will probably be higher than foods that are easier to make. When you prepare for the day, how long do you plan to prep the kitchen for? Are you a BBQ specialty food truck that requires 14 hours to smoke a meat before it's served? If so, that will also add to your operating and labor costs.

· **Market Changes:** As you might have seen in the last few years, certain food items have gone up in cost. Avocados are now more expensive and harder to find in comparison to a decade ago. Seafood prices are constantly changing, especially for larger fish like yellowtail and swordfish. It is important that your food prices change with the market to help you maintain a steady profit. If you plan on selling food items that change frequently, you might want to list your price as "Market price" or "Between $_ and $_" to get your customers used to the changes. This is a common practice for seafood sellers.

· **What type of food is it?** People are more inclined to spend more money on an upscale entrée or a large appetizer than they are to spend on a small dessert. It might be a good idea to ask yourself what kind of item you are pricing—if the item is something people will be less inclined to purchase, you might want to make the profit margin smaller and rely on the profit of other items to help bring in an income.

· **When do you plan on serving that food?** You need to take into account the mealtime in addition to the production costs. That is why so many restaurants offer a lunch serving size and a dinner serving size. If you are selling an item during lunch, you will need to take that into account. People are less inclined to spend more money on a lunch item than they would for the same item during dinner time. If you are serving something for lunch and offer it quickly, you might be able to get away with having a higher price because of the rush. So, take into account the meal period at which you plan to sell when deciding on your menu cost.

· **Think about your competition.** Is there another food truck in your area that sells similar food? If so, you don't necessarily need to lower your costs if theirs are lower; the key is to make sure you offer something they don't. Is there a way you can push your dish to become more desirable than the competitors? Can you offer an easy-to-make and cost-effective side dish? Is there an ingredient you can add in that will make it the better option? Find ways to beat your competitors in the factors outside of food costs, so you would be less likely to involve a strategy that might mean you lose profit.

· **Do you have sides, drinks, or desserts included?** This should also influence your costs. It might be a good idea to offer à la carte price and plate prices if your side items are more costly. Thinking back to our taco example, a side of jalapeños won't run you much, but if you are serving all of your tacos with beans and rice and not including that as a cost, you could be losing out on profit. The same should go for drinks. While a beverage may seem like a small cost for you to cover, the small cost will add up over time.

## In Conclusion

There are many factors to consider when pricing

out your menu. You will want to take the time to answer many of these questions for yourself, as it will help when it comes time to put your menu together. Also, don't be afraid to have multiple menu costs. If you have a lunch plate with a drink, that should be priced differently than a larger dinner portion with no drink. Food trucks change their prices much more commonly in comparison to brick and mortar restaurants, so feel free to follow this practice as well.

# HOW TO GET FUNDING

$S$urprisingly, financing a food truck is not as difficult as it might seem. Just about anyone can break into the food industry with a food truck—whether they stay and become successful is a different story, but with this book, I hope to give you a head start on the competition. Compared to brick and mortar restaurants, a food truck company can be started for as little as $30 to $40 thousand. There are many ways to go about financing your food truck, including options for those who have bad or fair credit. For example, you could begin by opting for a simpler life. Living frugal can allow you to save more money which you can invest in your food truck. Sell some of the things you no longer need in order to finance your business.

As you move forward in this chapter, I will share some advantages and disadvantages of each financing method, along with some key features that will hopefully help you decide which option is best for you.

## EQUIPMENT FINANCING

If you are trying to finance your food truck, or equipment to convert a van or a truck into a food truck, then the standard and most straightforward way to go is equipment financing. Equipment financing is typically a secured loan, meaning that it tends to come with lower interest rates, and the loan period tends to be on the longer side. The key with this type of loan is that it has to be used on *equipment*. You do not need outstanding or even good credit to qualify for these and, usually, people with fair credit can qualify with collateral. This is a good option for someone who is looking to start their business and who has little to no money to put toward purchasing the truck or major equipment. It will offer the lowest interest rates and, often, the longest loan terms, saving you thousands of dollars when compared to higher interest rate options. There will be some things they will want to see as part of your application, so be prepared. You may be asked to submit your annual salary, bank account statements to show your average balance, business plan, your credit report and score, among other things. Each lender will have slightly different requirements.

Some lenders who have better offers will ask that you make a certain yearly salary before you even apply, though there are still options for those with low credit. Usually a fair score of 650 is enough to qualify with some lenders, but your rates may be higher and your terms shorter, or you may need a cosigner. Keep in mind, that whenever you can produce a down payment or a cosigner, you will find the financing process easier, especially if you have low or fair credit. Starting a food truck business is a bold and exciting move, but do not be afraid to wait a little longer so you can build your credit, save for a down payment, and increase your chances of having a better loan option, especially if you think that doing so will be the best option for you in the long run. I have listed this financing option first because it is the best option to begin with as it will be the lowest risk of most of the options that follow.

### Business Line of Credit

A business line of credit gives you access to a specific amount of money to use as you would like. Unlike a credit card or a loan, it does not need to be limited to only credit card purchases or specific equipment purchases. A line of credit can be used as cash and can be accessed quickly. Upon approval, you would usually have access to the funds within a day, and for this method, you would typically take out a certain amount of money, then pay back the interest only on the amount you borrowed. A line of credit is a great option for business owners who are worried about running out of capital, may need money in emergency situations to keep their business running, or want to purchase items that can only be paid for with cash, such as a used food truck from a private vendor. The business line of credit can be used for a variety of business expenses, and it can vary from $10 thousand to up to $1 million, which makes it ideal for people who frequently have to make big purchases.

A business line of credit can be granted to people with low credit scores as well, and they are a great way to raise either or both your personal credit score or your business credit score. If you do have low or fair credit and are approved for a line of credit, be aware you will likely have to pay a larger interest rate. Typically, like the equipment loan, you will need to provide some form of collateral to be approved in this situation. In addition, because of the less strict regulations with lines of credit, you typically need to provide updated documents regarding income and expenses more frequently than other forms of financing. Unlike a loan, when you pay back the amount you used from the line of credit, you can continue using the line of credit as often as you need to. This makes it a form of revolving credit, which is a great tool to have when you are starting your business. If you are seeking out flexible financing that you can use again and again, then a business line of credit may be the best option for funding your food truck.

**SBA Microloan**

SBA stands for Small Business Administration. The SBA lends money to nonprofit businesses, and the nonprofit businesses that lend the money to small local businesses. These businesses are usually run by women, veterans, or other minority or marginalized groups, including low income households. These are a good option if the loan amount you need is less than $50,000, and can be used as capital, to buy equipment to start your business, purchase necessities, and pay for your food truck. These loans are typically given for up to six years and can have fairly affordable interest rates ranging from 5% up to 14%. These are a great option if your startup costs are on the lower side.

There are many advantages to SBA microloans. First of all, they are great for small food truck companies that do not anticipate paying a lot up front for things. You may already have a truck, but you need to update the equipment; in this case, SBA microloans are a great option. They are also a great choice for those who have limited credit history or work history, and they will work for anyone who plans on only having a limited number of employees.

These loans are granted by the "middleman," meaning that to receive one, you must find a local organization that grants them. For these microloans, smaller requirements are typically needed in comparison to the other financing options on this list. The business needs to be "for-profit," even though it is granted by a nonprofit. Because the nonprofits are accustomed to working with people who have had difficult situations in their lives, they do not necessarily require good credit (for example, some of these nonprofits have accepted scores as low as 580). You also don't need an extensive credit history or high income. There are three things they typically look for: first, they will want to know how you plan on paying the loan back. This means you will need to share your business plans and the amount you anticipate making. In addition, you need to have "good character," which means you can't have faced any serious charges in regard to dishonesty, like theft or burglary. You also need to have collateral. You will be asked to put your personal and business assets as collateral and, during the term of the loan, anything newly bought will also be used for this purpose.

. . .

## Business Credit Cards

A business credit card will work similarly to a personal credit card, in that you will have a revolving credit limit you can use continuously, a minimum payment due each month, an interest rate and associated fees, and it will require an application. There are many business credit cards available to you; although some will approve low credit scores, generally speaking, the better the credit score, the more likely you are to receive a good interest rate and a higher credit limit. A business credit card is a good option for financing food trucks, depending on how high your limit goes and how much you need to finance. Most business credit cards come with a promotional period where your interest rate is zero. You can take advantage of this by making larger purchases in your first year, then paying them off in larger monthly payments. So long as you pay it off before the end of the introductory period, you will end up paying nothing in interest rates.

A business credit card is a wonderful option for many people, but especially for anyone who has some money already saved and those with fairly good credit. The reason for this is simple: the rewards system. For people who already have money set aside, you can charge any large purchases on your business credit card, use the money you have set aside to pay it off quickly, pay the remainder before the promotional period is up, and then wind up saving a great deal of money throughout the ordeal. We mentioned before that you will be saving on interest rates, but more than that, you might actually save money on the purchase. Many business cards offer a cash back rewards program of 1%-2%, which means that when you pay it off, you would actually receive 1%-2% back from that purchase. While this will only be $1 out of a $100, it could wind up saving you a bigger sum of money on larger purchases. It's like a built-in coupon system—while these cards are great for any business owner to have, if your credit is fairly low, you might want to consider another option. The lower your credit score, the more likely you are to have a higher interest rate. If you do not pay off the amount within the promotional period, you could end up paying up to 20% of your purchase in interest fees.

## CROWDFUNDING

Crowdfunding is a great financing option for many people in today's world. It allows for multiple people to pool small amounts of money into helping advance a specific product or cause they believe in. For those who are already running a small private catering business, have large networks, or have already made their product known in some way, crowdfunding may be a great option. Crowdfunding usually involves signing up for a website like Indiegogo.com or Kickstarter.com or iFundWomen which targets women entrepreneurs only. Once you join, you would then give details about your business and what you hope to accomplish with the money you receive. It might also be a good idea to upload a video describing your mission, share some photos or business ideas, and give a set total you hope to reach. People who are interested in supporting you would then donate whatever amount they see fit. Typically, people who donate to these types of projects know they will not be receiving any product or service in exchange; as mentioned, they are usually donating because they believe in the service being offered.

Oculus has been one of the most legendary success story products using kickstarter. The virtual reality headset was created by Palmer Luckey who then went to Kickstarter to fundraise for funds to develop the product. Donations towards Oculus went way past its target of $250,000 and Facebook then went on to acquire the headset for the price of $2 billion. Palmer Luckey was only 21 years old when he developed the Oculus.

As with all financial options on this list, there are some advantages and disadvantages to this method. To begin, many crowdfunded campaigns fail for a variety of reasons, which is why it is important to choose the right website for your campaign, offer some type of reward (maybe small gift cards for those who make big donations), and market your food truck extensively and beyond merely creating the webpage. You need to share the campaign in as many ways as possible and with as many people as possible. There are a few different types of crowd-funding out there, and you will need to pick the one that works best for you. If you are trying to finance your food truck, it may be best to go with a donation or reward campaign. In the donation-based form, people donate without expecting anything in return. In the reward campaign, you offer set rewards for people who donate at a certain level.

**In Conclusion**

There are many options available to you for financing your food truck purchase. Even if you have saved the capital to purchase your food truck, it still might be worth looking into some of these financing options, so you can stock your truck and purchase your necessary items immediately and easily, or earn rewards through a business credit card. Now that you have an idea of where to begin in regard to financing, we will be moving on to Chapter Two: How to Price Your Menu.

**GET Your $397 Bonuses With This Link- https://bit.ly/2IlMu6l**

- Tax And Accounting Templates**($17 Value)**
- Bookkeeping Basics Tutorial Video**($47 Value)**
- Video Reveals  How To Save Hundreds Of Dollars With A Tax Firm **($63 Value)**
- Updates When New Food Truck Strategies Are Discovered!**($200 Value)**

# GENERAL MARKETING FOR A FOOD TRUCK

*O*ne area in which a food truck business owner can fail is with marketing. Before I get into the specifics of marketing your food truck after opening, let me touch a little on why marketing is crucial for your business to succeed.

## WHY IS MARKETING IMPORTANT?

Marketing, when done properly will guarantee you receive customers everyday. The key here is smart advertising which helps you to reach customers that otherwise wouldn't be in your radar. Here are four important areas that marketing helps the business:

1. **Builds the reputation**. Marketing is a huge part of building your reputation. For example, if you have a member of the team, like a Michelin star chef,

making the meals, you can use marketing to develop this aspect of your reputation. To build your reputation, focus your attention on the unique aspects of your food truck, from the menu to the people and, of course, the unique nuances in your service.

2. **Reaches out to customers**. Since your food truck has a specific customer base that you are reaching out to, it is crucial to advertise your services to them. The target audience will only know about your food truck if you have focused your marketing efforts toward reaching them. In 2010, a study by McKinsey & Company, a reputable American management consultancy firm, found that word of mouth was more powerful than ads.This is because people trusted the recommendation of a family member or a friend. In 2020, reliance on word of mouth to attract customers is still as effective according to a 2020 Nilesen report. However, because of game changers like social media and influencers, there is a need to complement it with ads. More people are spending time online and have access to advertisements that influence their spending trends. Having an ad online would give you an even wider reach than a traditional form of advertising.

3. **Gives a competitive edge**. Marketing gives you a competitive edge against your competition. Remember that your competition is also targeting your customers, so give your target audience more

information than your competitors to attract more customers from your general demographic. Lack of presence in the marketplace may appear as if your food truck is inferior to your competitor's.

4. **Drives up revenue**. The more people know about your food truck, the more revenue you are bound to get from it. Marketing helps people know about your business, and when they know about your products, they will be more likely to visit and spend money on your premises. Just make sure you live up to the expectations you have built up in your potential customers with your marketing.

### A FOOD TRUCK Marketing Strategy

All types of businesses need a marketing strategy, but food-related businesses face stiffer competition from each other because of the high demand for their products. You must understand that you will not only be competing against other food trucks, but also against restaurants, street food vendors, and other general food vendors in your locale.

Below I have listed four pillars of a marketing strategy that are sound for a food truck, so you can beat or, at the very least, be at par with the competition.

1. **Research your competition**. The market you are entering is already crowded,

which means you need to stand out—researching your competition will help you understand what works and what doesn't. The research should be on successful competition in the market that offers a similar menu to yours. You can also venture and research other restaurants in the locale that are doing well, even if they are not in your niche. Not only will you get some insight into what they are doing right to attract customers, but you would also gain a better understanding of your target market. This helps you tailor your marketing strategy to outshine the competition, while also appealing to your target market and remaining unique. It is crucial that you research your competition, so you can understand the loyalty of their customers better.

2. **Learn the target market**. Always remember that every food truck attracts specific customers because of their offerings, prices, and services. Obtaining some knowledge of your target market enables you to meet their needs and build loyalty; for example, finding out what their budget for eating out is, what they prefer to dine on, and what they look for

in a meal are all considerations you should be making while researching. This information is crucial for attracting the type of clientele you want and meeting your bottom line.

3. **Keep the clientele updated**. People prefer to buy from businesses where they feel they have a voice; therefore, you should keep the communication channels with your clientele open and two-way. When serving them, find out what you can do to make their experience at your food truck better. This may involve having a one-on-one with them while they eat the food or giving them a questionnaire to fill out. Better yet, take their email addresses and follow up with ALL your clients of the day who left emails. This enables you to keep tabs on the pulse of the business: the customers and what they want. Also, update clients of any new menus and menu items you create while striving to incorporate their suggestions where it is cost-effective and can work. If you are attending an event, like a concert or festival, and providing food, make sure you keep customers updated of your location so they can come over to visit your venue.

4. **Become part of the community**. It is easier for people to buy from locals that they trust, rather than from a stranger. So, build relationships with people you trust and contribute to the community around you. Provide meals during feeding programs, community fundraisers, and other events, and give discounts to local companies and organizations that you provide food to. This is a public relations stunt that can create the right kind of buzz that you would want around your food truck.

5. **Increase exposure**. Marketing and advertising opportunities are everywhere, as long as you know where to look. Hotel and motels (including Airbnb hosts) can allow you to leave your menu and any coupons you may have at their premises for the guests. Drop as many of these off as you can. You can also consider sponsoring a local event to increase your exposure. Another way to increase your exposure is to offer customers gift certificates. This is a highly effective marketing strategy because it compels one customer to buy a certificate for another, effectively inviting more people to your truck. Also, because food trucks can be

closer than a traditional restaurant,
offering people an entrée to entice them to
the truck is even easier.

6. **Excel at customer service**. Customers are your key to spreading word about your food truck without you having to spend a fortune. Word of mouth is only as good as the service you provide, and poor service will always have people turning away from your truck, no matter how great your food is. Keep the food truck clean, get the orders right, be expedient in giving the customer what they want, and have a friendly demeanor. These are standards that should be maintained, even as the traffic to your food truck increases with good customer reviews. Also make sure that your customer service gives you an edge over your competitors by giving them seamless support and access to your products and by having utmost quality control over what you offer them.

## MARKETING IDEAS for a Food Truck

When it comes to a food truck, sometimes grass-root marketing campaigns may be the best way to attract customers. This is mainly because your budget is less and they can be faster marketing campaigns to administer compared to more elaborate campaigns. I have collected some tried and tested grassroot campaigns for small businesses of this nature, which have proven to work remarkably well.

· **Offer a discount**. Small discounts are always a good idea in the food industry because they mitigate the reason a customer will choose another food truck over yours. People can never have enough discounts, and discounts are an excellent way to attract new customers and keep existing ones loyal. At the end of the day, it is all about customers, and they will go to a food truck where they can get value at a bargain. The trick is in how you present the discount; for example, a bowl of pasta can be presented merely as $8, or it can be presented as 20% off the usual price of $10. The meal costs $8 in both scenarios, but in the latter option, the customer becomes attracted by the slash in prices, which clearly shows that they have received a bargain for the meal.

· **Offer a special**. Reach out to certain influential members of the community with specials at first, just to get the ball rolling. If you are confident about the response of the general public toward the special, you can offer it to all your customers. By offering it to a select few in the community, you are also testing the waters to see how much goodwill and popularity the special will attain. Take the time to learn more about which milestones that are celebrated by everyone in the community. For example, the anniversary of an event or recognition of a person are great days to have a special in honor of the event.

· **Referrals**. Grassroot marketing works in conjunction with a word of mouth and is an inexpensive way to find more customers for your food truck. Give the existing customers an incentive to invite more of their friends, which can be in the form of a coupon or an entrance into a prize draw. Use social media channels like Facebook and Twitter to spread the news about your food truck and encourage your customers to share your links with friends and family.

· **Go out**. Being a food truck permits you to move around and go to the customer instead of waiting for the customer to come to you. Earlier, I talked about attending events, providing food, and inviting your customers to the venue. Even if your customers don't come around, you have moved to the center of the action and gone to another customer pool. Fairs, festivals, and other community events are great places to set up camp when looking for customers.

· **Partner with organizations**. Provide food for charity organizations with events and conferences, but apart from providing food, you can also contribute your time and effort to local charity causes, so you can build solid relations. You can share your profits after hosting a fundraising event with the cause of your choice—just make sure the cause is local if you want to have the most impact.

· **Loyalty programs**. Having a loyalty program may seem a little over the top for a food truck, but it really isn't if you have plans for expansion. Create an online food app that can help you amass the following you are looking for. Also, start collecting emails early and plan to create your own loyalty club for when you have expanded. In the meantime, you can merge your online food app with existing loyalty programs in local hotels and motels to give your food truck more visibility.

### The Best Online tools for Marketing Your Food Truck

### Instagram

Instagram is a food business's best friend. For foodies, instagram is addictive, and the way people have been surfing the site and looking at food pictures led to the coining of the term *food porn*. For the purposes of marketing, ignore the offensiveness of the term and focus on the concept behind it —*millions* of people post pictures of meals they are having at one restaurant or another, and you can easily use the same platform to showcase your menu and entice customers to your truck with mouthwatering photos.

Posting high quality photos of your food online is one of the best ways you can promote your food truck, but make sure you keep your food truck's Instagram account strictly business and devoid of any personal photos. This will give it the professional and serious feel you want for your truck.

When taking the photos, make sure you do it using natural lighting, while also keeping the backlight bright. Use angles to get the best shot and make the food look larger than life. The softer and more balanced the lighting, the more attractive and appetizing the food will appear on your Instagram page.

## YELP

This is one of the most powerful online tools to be used in the food industry. The reason for that is because Yelp receives a lot of traffic since it features reviews from real customers. The site almost has 150 million people visiting it per month, so if you have your food truck listed as business on Yelp, you can receive a lot of exposure.

On Yelp, you are reaching out to people who are ready to buy and don't need further convincing. Most people you reach on the site are looking at your reviews and menu to determine the quality of your product. Positive reviews about your food truck on Yelp will help drive traffic to your business.

Plus, Yelp displays one or two ads per customer search, giving your business the exposure it needs to drive revenue up. It can help you to get noticed locally, unlike other paid online services. The platform also allows customers to order online, increasing the chances of making a sale. The chances of a customer changing their mind when they have to travel physically to your food truck are higher compared to them cancelling an online order.

The only setback with Yelp is that some business owners have flagged certain reviews as false, but the site has regulations that allow the review to stay up unless it has contravened the site's terms of service. Unfortunately, you can get reviewed on Yelp even without having an account. To mitigate poor reviews, it is important to have a Yelp account and take control of the reviews. This can help you counter any negative feedback and keep communication lines with reviewers open.

Yelp will eliminate any competitive profiles on your profile, allowing you to stand out. Just make sure you place as many of your details as possible on the site, which would include your typical locations on different days, menu, price range, and hours of operation. Of course, remember to post plenty of high quality photos.

· · ·

## GOOGLE+

This is a highly effective social network operated by Google. Google is the search engine, whereas Google+ is the social media site, similar to Facebook and Twitter. Google+ allows you to host hangouts on their site and use content to market to your customer base. The site features a +1 button on the page to help the customer promote your product to others who enjoy similar products.

By allowing you to host a hangout the platform facilitates deeper engagement between you, your customers, and other stakeholders. You get to build your reputation online while you drive the traffic to your business. You can answer customer questions about your menu, ingredients, and even have contests and giveaways. Although you may not get as wide an audience as Facebook and Twitter, you can still have a sizable target audience. Just maintain a presence on the bigger social media channels for even wider reach.

Enable Google alerts, which will let you know when your food truck name appears in any content piece on the web. This way, you can keep track of who is talking about you and partner with them for even more exposure.

## Facebook

Facebook has always been on the forefront of

offering unique marketing opportunities to small businesses, which can include your food truck. One of the unique aspects of Facebook is that it is not a place for the hard sell—keep that angle for traditional advertising, like radio and TV. Hard selling on Facebook includes repeating your slogan over and over, posting repetitive content about your food truck, and giving your audience lists and prices without any real content or conversation. People will unfollow you because they find your page boring and aggressive, and you would have no real connection with them.

Instead, use soft sale tactics like having conversations with people and posting videos and photos. This is a fun and relaxed way to market people have fun looking at your content, as well as yourself. Soft selling is all about having fun with the customer and compelling them to buy without marketing yourself too aggressively. With Facebook, you have to post relevant content frequently while updating your audience on events, changes in venue, and new items on the menu. Having said that, only post when you have interesting content—not daily for the sake of it. This means the onus is on you to find interesting content to post regularly. Keep in mind Facebook users usually check their feeds at least 25 times a week.

For you to succeed in marketing on Facebook, you need to reply to comments on your content quickly and encourage even more comments; a 24-hour response time is best. If you fail to respond on time, you will gradually lose the friends and followers you have amassed. Using tools like Facebook Insights will help you learn more about your customers. The information you can get will help you create even better content for your audience.

## TWITTER

The golden rule when using Twitter is to use it as the front door into your marketing efforts. Twitter is not a social media network for your food truck business, but rather for news and information. It is where you would go to meet potential customers and other stakeholders, have a chat to break the ice, and connect with them enough to invite them to follow you on other channels where you would have more in-depth content.

When using Twitter, you must have a brand-centric profile; this is not the place to use your nickname or your pet's name. You want the profile to be immediately recognizable to the target market at first glance. With it, write a concise and clear bio in less than 160 characters to describe your products and services. Make sure to include a link to your website in this section as well.

Once this is done, you can begin to use Twitter wools like HootSuite and Sprout Social to find tweets related to your industry and see what people are talking about. These tools will also help you find tweets about your food truck, so you can interact and respond to followers in a timely fashion. Always maintain a professional approach when replying to tweets from your customer base, whether negative or positive.

Keep in mind that tweets are more ephemeral in nature compared to posts, so reply to any of them quickly so you don't miss your window of opportunity for an interaction. When it comes to your own tweets, keep them coming regularly to your audience so you can remain relevant. Twitter comes with an internal analytics tool that will help you determine the best frequency for posting. Just remember to keep the tweets short and with the front door nature of the platform. Nevertheless, invite your audience to check out longer posts on your website and Facebook page.

THERE IS much to be said about using these online tools to market your food truck but here is the take away I want you to remember when it comes to using them: you must create a content plan and find influencers to help you achieve your goals.

Having a content plan allows you to be systematic about the information you dispatch to your target market. Mondays can be the days when you feature special promotions and Tuesdays can be for photos and videos. Wednesdays can be more content-intensive, with informative tips for making certain recipes you feature on your menu at home. Thursdays would be for keeping it light with high-lights about trending industry news and new food trends. On Friday, you can keep the focus on the customers and employees.

Finding and following influencers in your niche is a great way to build authority and credibility with the right customer base. Engage with them and find out how you can partner. Doing so would allow you to have access to their already established following and grow your own reputation and brand. Use tools like Twellow, Klout, and Commun.it to find the influence of your followers, then choose those with the greatest authority and engage. Also, establish whom you should follow by looking at their responses to your content, knowledge of the indus-try, and relevance to the food truck business community. Following everyone who follows you can jumble up your feeds and compromise your relevance, so make sure to be a bit choosy here.

Always remember to share any links that mention your business or feature you on the above online platforms, so you can stay relevant. They would also help you get the attention of journalists and food bloggers in your locale.

. . .

## WEBSITE

Don't forget to invest in your own website. Owning a website is crucial to maintaining an online presence and marketing to them. On a website, you can have in-depth content that adds value to your customer and establishes you as an authority. Being available online makes you available to customers using search engines when they are searching for a place to eat. Statistics show that 93% of purchase decisions begin with a search engine. That includes decisions about where to spend money when eating out.

## FOOD TRUCK MARKETING Dos and Don'ts

The food truck phenomenon has been growing steadily over the last decade, and even though it may sound simple from the name, it is far from it. Many people believe that running a food truck is about fueling a truck, getting some supplies, and serving people food as you go. The scenario on the ground is much more different, which is why this niche comes with definite dos and don'ts, especially when marketing.

## The Dos

· **Get a memorable name**. Memorable names remain in your customer's memory for longer. The name should have an element of food in them and be able to conjure the image of something delicious. Consider names like "cupcake haven," "the bon bon chariot," or "the tasty taco truck," for example. The above names are food-oriented, but you can also consider the name from your locale, the signature dish that defines your business, or even your own name. For example, there are options like "the Torres Tasty Taco," "Bob's Bon Bon Chariot," or "New York Chimichanga." If you offer a specialty food like a burger or Italian cuisine, consider naming the truck after your specialty; for example, "A Mexican Chiquita's Pot."

· **Have set venues**. You don't have to stay in one place, but if you are moving around on different days have consistent locations where your regular customers can find you, post a regular schedule on your website and make sure you are near a place where people can find a seating area to enjoy your dish. The aim of choosing such a location is to make sure your customers are comfortable without spending too much money, so choose your spots wisely. If you can't find such a place, come with some few portable chairs and tables of your own and set up for your customers.

· **Play music**. A food truck is typically associated with fun and festivity. Maintain an air of cheeriness and charm with some relevant music. The music doesn't have to be thematic to the food truck cuisine, like mariachi music for a burrito or taco truck. Instead, you can have cosmopolitan music to attract all types of customers. Most cuisines have gained a universal following, even though they are native to certain people of the world. However, if you want to maintain the authenticity of your cuisine and brand, you can try playing native music. It may attract people from all walks of life who are curious to sample a new culture. When it comes to playing music, especially in a public space, it is crucial to keep the tunes audible but not obnoxious. In the example of a Mexican-themed food truck, having a mariachi band that plays at selected times to entertain customers is fine, and they would also have to be restrained in their performance. However, it is unacceptable to blare music non-stop in a public place and disrupt the peace. The aim of the music is to attract and keep customers entertained.

· **Be friendly**. Perhaps the most significant marketing strategy you can employ as the owner of a food truck is to be personable with your customers. This strategy will work on both your customers and fellow food truckers. It also allows you to become part of the food industry and community in your locale, and your customers will come to appreciate friendly service. It is essential that you maintain good—if not great—relations with fellow food truckers because it facilitates the flow of information regarding updates in regulations, upcoming events, newly found hot spots, and even just for safety purposes. The food truck business is not suited to a lone wolf.

· **Avoid dirt**. The cleanliness of your truck may seem like just a sanitary issue, but it should also be treated as a significant part of your marketing strategy. Customers will only buy from a clean truck where both the vehicle and the person are clean. A filthy truck will kill your marketing efforts, as will customers spotting pests like cockroaches or rats. Plus, it will keep authorities away, as word travels fast if you have trouble with the authorities about the cleanliness of your truck. Nobody will want to buy from you in that case, no matter how hard you try to rebrand yourself.

## The Don'ts

· **Overcharge**. The pricing you put on your products is an excellent way to indirectly market your food truck. People like bargains and will flock to a place with an affordable process and great value. Please note that I said affordable—*not* dirt cheap because not only do you have a bottom line to meet, but also sometimes appearing cheap can make it seem like your products are of lower quality. Find a balance by checking out with your competitors' prices and offer prices that are competitive within that range. It doesn't matter how exceptional or swanky your food or food truck is; you are still serving food out of a truck and your prices should match your niche. Setting the prices for your food should be a shrewd but realistic affair that meets both your and your customer's needs. Keep your prices reasonable and food excellent, and you will have a winning marketing strategy.

· **Be over-the-top**. Marketing is about maximizing your profit without affecting your budget. Unfortunately, an over-the-top and fanciful food truck is not a great marketing gimmick because it takes a lot of financing to make the truck fancy. All the bells and whistles do not guarantee profits. Keep it simple and functional; a great design is acceptable, but concentrate your efforts on the food and service, which will market you even better. Speaking of food and service, don't go over the top in this area either. The point of a food truck is for the customer to grab something quick, delicious, and convenient for them. If they have to use a knife and fork for the meal, it may have no place in a food truck menu. Focus on providing your customers with good and fast food and an inviting ambiance and vibe, and you will win. Over-the-top service is having multiple servers in the small confined space. That is not a good look, as the truck will look overcrowded and customers will not enjoy the many bodies so close to them while they try to eat. Consider one cook who can multitask and serve with a smile. Overcrowding gives the impression of chaos, whereas having fewer staff can give the impression of a neat and organized space. Appearance is everything in marketing, and over-the-top isn't always a successful marketing strategy. Simple and effective would work better.

## Mobile Food Trends to Focus Your Marketing Strategies on

The food truck industry has been maturing since it became popular nearly a decade ago. With its popularity come trends that food truck owners can take advantage of to market their businesses. These trends include:

· **Food truck eateries**. Food trucks no longer need to be solitary businesses in the open air waiting for customers. Truck yards are now organizing indoor food truck eateries where several food trucks are can in warehouses or similar facilities to serve food. Within this space, they share room with bars, live bands, and various games. This concept allows food truck owners to have access to customers, and customers can access their favorite food trucks easily. This trend has been picking up speed as more truck yards and places like county fairs open their spaces to facilitate this dining experience. During these sessions, the customers can experience unusual foods like pizza with snake or alligator meat toppings. Come up with your own special menu and join one of these eateries to draw in more customers. Success stories of food truck eateries, like the Seventh Street Truck Park in Minnesota, have sparked a revolution in the food truck industry and inspired many more eateries to be formed.

· **Specialty drinks**. Specialty drinks are a huge trend right now, which you can incorporate into your menu to attract even more customers. Now, people don't have to go to an upscale establishment to have upscale beverages. These kinds of drinks can include homemade lemonades with a unique twist, specialty ice creams, or premium teas, all of which can be quite profitable as well. This is a niche you can focus on to draw in more customers who will also sample your dishes.

· **Attend private events**. The trend of having food trucks at events like bar mitzvahs, weddings, and graduations is on the rise as millenials move away from the typical traditional catering. To access such events, make sure you share your portfolio with wedding planners, universities, churches, and synagogues. Such events typically have 200 to 300 people and are great places to market your products and services, so you can gain more clients.

· **Offer free WiFi**. Technology is helping in keeping food trucks relevant and more efficient. This makes the customers want to buy from your truck, as they can gain access to free WiFi with their meal, giving you an edge on your competition. It may cost you slightly more, but you would build a reputation and customers will continue to come back.

SUPERFAST MENUS ARE BECOMING INCREASINGLY popular, and food trucks are the best place to get a quick meal on the go. This means that food trucks are not waning in popularity, but there is a need to utilize smart marketing to maximize their potential.

# HOW TO WRITE A BUSINESS PLAN

*A* business plan is essential before beginning your food truck and is often needed to help secure financing. However, a business plan isn't only helpful for convincing others why your business will do well; oftentimes, a business plan can help you finalize details you had not even thought about. A business plan will give you clear goals and will help you narrow down the details if you feel caught between choices. It will also help you decide what your customer demographics will be and will give you information to make the most profitable choices. This chapter will go over each important section of a business plan. I will also guide you by asking questions so you can fill in the details. Once you have a business plan, you can then use it to try to gain investors or simply have a guide to a more successful business.

.  .  .

## Executive Summary

This is the first part of your business plan and will serve as an introduction for the reader. You will want this section to be concise and intriguing, while answering some important questions at the same time. This is where you can introduce your company and its personality, along with sharing your anticipated plans and why you believe you will be successful. It is here that you will also introduce your market, background information, knowledge, and goals as a company. Although this is technically the first section of the business plan, I actually recommend you write it *last*. Summaries are much easier to write once you have laid out every detail; only then can you concisely answer the necessary questions. Executive summaries tend to be around one page in length. Here are some key things you need to include in it:

· **Overview**: In the first few sentences, you will want to give your name and the name of your food truck. Discuss why you are starting a food truck business and explain where you plan to work primarily (the main city or county).

· **Product**: This is your opportunity to introduce your plans for your menu. Share what cuisine or item you plan to serve and the ways your food truck would provide something that may not be readily available. You will also need to explain how you plan on selling the food. Are you only selling from the food truck? Do you plan on catering? Do you have a restaurant as well? Do not be too in-depth about the food, as you will have a chance to talk about that later on.

· **Financing**: Share briefly how much money you anticipate needing early on, along with what you plan to do with that money. There is a longer financial section later, so you won't need to add too much detail in this short paragraph. This section should serve merely as an introduction to the financials.

· **Mission statement**: Give the reader the heart of your business. Why did you decide to start a food truck? Why are you opening one with this specific menu? What is it you hope to accomplish? What do you want your customer to walk away with? This is also important information for you to know and figure out.

· **Management team**: Readers will want to know who will be running the food truck. Do you have any business partners? Do you plan on hiring a manager, in addition to yourself? Are you working with family? This is where you would give information about who would be keeping the business functioning.

· **Sales forecast**: This will be very important for

potential investors. Describe your first-year costs and your expected sales. People will want to know how much you plan and hope to make your first year, and if it is a reasonable estimate. Be sure to be realistic here; don't put down an income that can only be made by working 24 hours a day. Aim for an estimate that is slightly more than conservative.

· **Expansion plan**: Have you thought about what you want for your food truck's future? Consider if you are hoping to expand to a full-scale restaurant. Maybe you want to open a second truck or start a catering business. Whatever you hope to accomplish, this section is where you will want to describe your goal.

THE EXECUTIVE SUMMARY should give an idea of why your business is needed and what you would provide as a business. These are details you should know easily and should have decided prior to beginning your business.

### COMPANY DESCRIPTION

This is the section where you will provide more details about your truck and its theme. You will share the purpose of the food truck while also discussing how it will play a part in your community (for example, will it be the only Thai food place open for lunch in a business area?). Share all the ways your food truck participates with the community. For example, if you have a farm-fresh menu and you plan on sourcing your ingredients from a local farm, this spot is a good place to say that. If you plan on being an affordable and quick option for a busy neighborhood or university town, then share those details. Think of all the ways your food truck will add to the local community. This is also where you should talk about your ideal customer and how you plan to win them over. For example, if you have a farm-fresh food truck, you will want to reach a customer who cares about the ingredients they consume and who has the finances to pay for higher quality ingredients. How will you win them over? Perhaps you are using eco-conscious materials as well. If you plan on selling to special events or catering, you will want to give more details about that in this area as well.

This is the part of the business plan where you will be giving your plan of what you want to do with your food truck and how you plan to do it. It is all about what you want to accomplish most in your daily operations. You might also want to introduce how your food truck will stand out from its competitors; don't be afraid to share how your food truck will be different. Uniqueness could help you in this case. Aside from the financial section, this is the part that can help sell your food truck to your investors.

You can also ask yourself the following questions before you begin writing this section: Why am I opening a food truck and not a restaurant? Where will I prepare for the day? How will I compete with local restaurants? What niche am I serving? What is my food truck's advantage?

## Business Operations

This section would be all about setting up your food truck, and you will want to share a list of what needs to be done before you begin your business. Make a list of all of the equipment and supplies that you will need, as well as your main hours of operation. You don't need to go into details about the expenses; just the items and tasks themselves. This section will also cover all of your daily plans for your food truck business. Provide notes detailing how many days of the week you plan to be open, and how many shifts per day you will have. Make sure you also describe how you plan on preparing food for your shifts. Will you make the food on site and open at a certain time? Will you be delivering hot and prepared food?

You will also want to share all that your food truck will do. If you plan on selling drinks and desserts, describe that. Where do you plan to set up?

This is a good section to share where you plan on selling your food. Give as many location ideas as you can get. If you need to include a map, feel free to do so. If you will have routine locations, give those as well. You should share who you have hired or, if you still need to hire employees, how many people you plan on hiring. You will want to share whether you plan on having full-time employees or only part-time employees. It might be a good idea to also share how many hours you hope each employee would work each week. Also be sure to include if you plan on hiring more people in the future after your first six months.

Finally, this is the part of the business plan where you can provide details about your menu. Do you have a signature item? Describe it along with the key ingredients, and also give your sources for those ingredients. If you plan on having seasonal items on the menu, you might want to mention those, as it will help your reader know you have planned ahead.

## MARKET ANALYSIS

This is the section of the business plan where you will share your reasons for starting a food truck, and why you believe your food truck will succeed based on what you have seen in the food truck market. Everything that is in this section should aim to prove that you will be successful. You will need a market analysis from your target location, data about trends, and information from other relevant sources.

Here is where you should also share your ideal demographic and why you expect them to eat at your food truck. You will want to share the preferences of your ideal customers and use research to help make valid points, with part of your research including findings from local restaurants. Feel free to reach out to other food trucks from similar cities to ask about their customer demographics or even your chamber of commerce, as the latter would often know about business needs and may be able to tell you where your food truck can be successful. For this section of the business plan, you may want to mention any community centers or schools that may be willing to partner with you. If you have businesses who are willing to let you park in their space, talk about that here too.

Finally, you will want to talk about your competition in this section. A business plan should anticipate any potential roadblocks and show how you plan to work through them. Show how you plan to succeed even with competitors. This section will probably be the most research-heavy section you will need to write.

## MARKETING

A food truck business will need to rely heavily on

marketing to succeed. In this section, you will need to describe in detail how you plan to promote and market your business. There are key things your readers will want to know about when it comes to marketing:

· **Your food truck design**: Investors will want to know what will make your food truck stand out, and that should be something you should know as well. What design goal do you have for your food truck?

· **Your website**: When will you launch your website? What will you have on it? You need to keep your website up-to-date, and your readers will want to see that information included in your marketing plan. Do you plan on keeping the menu updated? Will you put your locations online? What other information do you need to provide?

· **Associations or city-related directories**: Are you planning on being involved with any food truck associations or organizations? Will you be added to your city's business directory? Where do you plan to make your business known professionally?

· **Social media**: This section is important for a food truck business, and potential investors will need to see that you have thought about incorporating social media into your plan. Twitter, Facebook, and Instagram are the most active social media websites for food trucks. How do you plan on using social media to generate interest? What information do you plan on sharing? How do you plan on growing your social media following?

· **Television**: Have you researched any potential avenues for promoting yourself on television? Can you make an appearance on local city news? Many news networks share new businesses and may be interested in featuring yours, but you will have to reach out.

· **Community events**: Do you plan to associate with and participate in any community events? In what ways do you hope to make your business known locally?

IN SHORT, this section is all about proving you are willing to do whatever you can to make your food truck business known. Take the time to research all the ways you can do this and share your plans for marketing.

## SALES

Aside from the financial aspect that will come later in the business plan, this will be important—you need to give detailed information about your sales. You need to figure out exactly how much you must sell to keep your business running, which includes the cost for all ingredients, the truck, and your employees. It will be how much you will need to make to break even. Then, you need to figure out how much you need to sell to make a true profit. A profit would be more than you pay yourself in wages. You will want to have an idea of your menu prices and explain them in this section. All of this information will also be useful for you, so you can have monthly, weekly, and daily targets to hit.

### FINANCIAL PROJECTIONS

This will likely be the most important part of your business plan, in addition to the executive summary. It is important to set financial goals for yourself that are clear and reasonable. While it might be difficult to think about your projections before you even begin your business, doing so will force you to learn how to allocate your money properly, along with helping you stay more organized. Here are a few key points you should include:

· **Estimated costs to open**: You need to show how much money it will cost to get your business up and running. How much will you need for ingredients? Do you have a budget for your truck? How much do you need to allocate for the first month or two? These are all things you need to plan for as part of your startup costs.

· **Supplies and equipment**: In addition to the start-up costs, you will want to have a section that focuses strictly on equipment and supplies. Think small supplies like plates and such, along with big supplies like oven and fryer.

· **Employee costs**: How much do you plan to pay yourself when your business first opens? How much will it cost to pay your employees for the first three months? Do you need to pay accountants, tax specialists, or any fees associated with opening your food truck? Include every detail you can.

· **Estimated other costs**: How much should you include for food that is returned or has gone to waste? What about vehicle maintenance? Do you plan on having money set aside for repairs in case something comes up within the first few months? What about insurance costs?

· **First year projections**: You will want to break down your first-year projections into quarterly and monthly projections. In this spot, incorporate all income, costs, and losses over the first year. At this stage, you only need to think about one-year projections and not beyond that. It is essential you take the time to really figure out how much money it will cost to keep your food truck running, as you don't want to have to shut your business down early just because you forgot to include employee wages.

**Appendix**

This is the section where you will include any additional information that does not fit in any of the others. Here, you can include design mock ups of your truck (or photos if you have it already), any other concepts (menu mockups, recipes), legal or licensing documents you have already obtained, letters of reference, research materials, and anything else you deem necessary.

## In Conclusion

As you can see, a business plan is essential not only to share with investors, but for yourself as a new food truck owner. By going through and filling in the business plan, you will gain a true understanding of all you need to keep your business open, along with what you need to succeed. While it may seem like a lot of information, with the guidance of this chapter, you now have a clear idea of what you need to do to gather that information.

# HOW TO HIRE GOOD WORKERS

One of the most important steps you will make shortly before you begin running your food truck will be to hire workers. This chapter assumes that you will not be hiring people you know to help you run the food truck. In this part of the book, I will go over how to help you decide how many employees you will need, what roles you need to fill in your new business, and give you advice on hiring trustworthy employees. The previous chapters should have given you a vague idea of how many hours you would like to run on a weekly basis and what shifts you need to fill. However, there are other things you need to consider. Do you plan on being at the food truck any time it is open? Will you have someone to oversee it when you are unwell or cannot oversee it? What role are you going to fill? These are questions that will hopefully get you thinking about the importance of staffing when it comes to opening a food truck business. Most food trucks have between 2-7 employees working on the truck, in the commercial kitchen, and offsite.

### DETERMINE YOUR FOOD Truck Staffing Needs

The most important step before you begin the process of hiring is to determine what you need in terms of staff. To help you figure this out, I will be running you through a list of roles you may have to fill. Here is where you would decide if you are going to fill one role permanently and every time the truck is open, or if you plan to work as a floater, going wherever you're needed for the day.

### ONSITE VS OFFSITE

Chances are, you will not only need to hire employees to work *at* the food truck, but you will likely need to hire employees to work *outside* the food truck's operating hours. This is what I mean by onsite vs offsite. Let's begin with onsite jobs as they are likely the easiest to decide first.

### ONSITE—CASHIER/WINDOW Attendant

You will need to have an employee whose focus for the shift is to take orders and/or to process payments. Some businesses take orders first, then process the payment once the food is ready. I recommend settling the cost with the order. The window attendant will need to have a friendly attitude and great customer service skills. They will need to be knowledgeable about the menu, so they can answer questions for potential customers. The window person will likely be the one who handles the drink orders as well, whether that be pouring drinks or handing the customer a bottled beverage. Typically, it is not wise to have a cook take the orders, especially during busy hours. The chef and cooks will likely be too busy processing orders to take the time needed to answer questions or provide quality customer service.

### ONSITE—FOOD **Truck Driver** *(possibly)*

Depending on the type of vehicle you choose to invest in, you may or may not necessarily need a bus driver. If you choose to start a bustaurant, you will need to either be commercially licensed or hire someone to drive during shift hours. If you are licensed to drive your vehicle, you will probably not need to worry about this concern, but it is worth mentioning and thinking about. Be sure to check if you are licensed to drive your vehicle before scheduling your first shifts.

. . .

### ONSITE — MANAGER (*possibly*)

As mentioned, you will need to decide if you will be the person who oversees every shift, or if you plan to hire a manager to do that on your off shifts. Many people prefer to oversee every shift when they first begin, but this practice usually cannot be continued long term, especially if you plan on working multiple shifts in one day. If you choose to specialize in lunch hour meals and you only work lunch shifts and take a day or two off, you may be able to manage working without a manager; however, it is important you keep your goals realistic. How much can you work initially, and how much do you want to work after the first three months? As the main manager, your duties will involve opening the food truck and shutting it down, along with making inventory purchases, keeping track of inventory, and, if you choose, organizing the menu. For those who choose to hire an additional manager, you will want to make sure your manager has experience running either a food truck or a restaurant. They will need to learn how to fill every role in and out of the food truck to ensure they can help the team succeed in your absence.

### ONSITE — CHEF and Cook

The chef will be one of the most important employees in your business. Many people who start a food truck business do so because they enjoy cooking, but you need to keep in mind that if you plan to run the business and cook, you will likely still need to hire a chef. These are the workers who will be running your kitchen and making sure everything is going smoothly. Given how much work you will have to manage and how many employees you will have to direct, you will need someone who can manage the kitchen area as well. If you decide not to cook at all, this employee will be even more valuable. While you, as the owner, will oversee the menu, the chef should be the one who suggests the menu items and specials, and ultimately decides the menu. If you do not plan on being the head chef yourself, you need to keep in mind that the menu would become the chef's specialty. While you may have some disagreements, you should remember they only want to show off the food and help the truck succeed. When you hire a chef, aim to hire someone who has experience in a fast-paced kitchen.

IN ADDITION TO A CHEF, you will likely need to hire a cook as well. Cooks are the people who will prep the food and generally follow the chef's instruction. Cooks need to be hardworking, and need to be able to work well with the chef, the latter of whom would also be in charge of overseeing the cooks' training. Having a skilled cook, as well as a responsible chef, will definitely help make your kitchen run smoother. It is possible to get by with only a cook or a chef, especially if you plan on filling one of those roles, but depending on the size of your food truck business, you should consider hiring both.

### ONSITE AND OFFSITE—KITCHEN Workers

The kitchen workers are anyone who helps in regard to kitchen duties. You might need to hire one or more of these workers. The kitchen workers may handle prep work, garnishes, salads, soups, or any small kitchen tasks that can be done without culinary experience. Kitchen workers will help your cook and chef move much quickly. These workers can also be cross trained to handle other tasks, such as window service and cash handling. Your kitchen worker may work onsite to help during a service period, or they may work off site to prepare things for the day. You will want to hire someone who has experience or is easily trainable. Entry level kitchen workers often handle dish duties, loading and unloading, among other tasks that shouldn't usually be left for the chef or cook. You will want to hire 2-3 if you plan on running a full-time operation.

### OFFSITE—BOOKKEEPING

Unless you yourself are an accountant, or have

accounting and tax experience, you will want to look into hiring a bookkeeper. In the beginning you are going to need to keep track of how well you are doing financially. The first few months are crucial. You need to stay up to date with your profits so you can make changes early on if needed. You also need to make sure you are making enough to pay your workers, buy ingredients, and pay back any loans that you took out to finance your business.

**Hiring Good Employees**

Once you decide how many employees you need to hire for a successful food truck business, you will need to begin the hiring process. However, it's not just about jumping in and hiring anyone who wants to work for you—you need to be focused and know exactly what you are looking for before you begin. I will guide you through a few simple steps to help you decide what kind of employees you need and decipher whether the person you are considering is fit for the job.

1. **Decide on your requirements:** You have specific needs in mind, especially since you are operating out of a truck and not a brick and mortar building.

a. **Physical requirements:** You need people who can do certain physical activities for a long time.

Typically, your shifts will require people to be standing for most of their time, so be straightforward about that and list it as a physical requirement. You will probably need people who can work in hot environments, given how warm a kitchen environment can get.

b. **Experience:** Depending on the role you are filling; you will likely want someone with experience working in a fast-paced kitchen environment. If you are hiring kitchen workers and are open to entry level, you can also add that experience is preferred, but not necessary. It is important to think about the kind of experience you want as well; many people list "culinary degree required" for their food truck job and receive many certified applicants, but there are also numerous food truck cooks who have extensive experience who never went to culinary school. If your menu is complicated or features only vegan or farm fresh foods, perhaps seek out someone who has experience in those fields, even if they have not pursued a degree.

c. **Behavior:** You will want to hire someone who has the ability to work well in a team environment, considering how close the employees will be working with each other and how small the business is. Tasks and knowledge can be taught, but work ethic and behaviors cannot be.

d. **Familiarity and Intelligence:** You do not necessarily need someone who has a college degree, so long as the person is a quick learner and catches on early. This might be hard to gauge until you start training, which is why you should always have a trial run for a week or two before the official position is offered. You can also ask people if they are familiar with the cuisine you offer if that feels necessary to you.

2. **Know what you can offer your employee:** Decide what you can feasibly afford to spend on your employees and ration it out accordingly. At the same time, do not offer a wage that is so low that you cannot get a qualified employee, or so low that your employees wind up having to work three jobs to survive. You are running a business with people; if you need a qualified chef but are open to training new employees in other aspects, be willing to pay a higher salary to the chef. If your dishes are not overly complicated, consider hiring an entry level cook and giving better wages to all of your employees. Also, do not say you might offer something in the future if you do not know whether you will or won't, especially as it relates to insurance benefits.

3. **Expand your network:** While some of your employees may be family or friends, consider expanding your network too. It is nice to be able to work with family and friends, but it also puts a lot of pressure on them to learn things they might not be all that familiar with. While they can help you get the food truck business set up, consider expanding

beyond your personal network. It will save you time and pressure during the transition period.

4. **Conduct background checks:** It is always a good idea to conduct a background check on potential employees, as it will tell you if the prospect has had any bad experiences with old jobs, or if they have a criminal record of any kind. This is not to say that you should not consider hiring people who have committed crimes; that is entirely up to you. However, it is good to know before you make your decision. There have been numerous companies who have hired entire staff of previous felons because they understand second chances and know that many people with these pasts are willing to work harder than people who haven't been through that experience. Whatever choice you make, a background check will give you the opportunity to have an open conversation.

5. **Test out your potential employees:** Given the nature of the food truck business, it is acceptable to have a trial run with your employees. If you are hiring kitchen workers and don't know how well someone can learn, consider giving them a prep shift. See if they do well and pick up quickly, and be sure to pay them, even if it is a trial period. If you want to see how skilled a cook or chef is, hire them to make sample dishes and have them invent an item for the menu. Try different methods to determine who you want working for your business.

. . .

**Let Me Give You a Little Story...**

I was giving business advice to an owner of a new food truck that specialized in fun and unique sandwich combinations. The person had hired a family member to work as a manager for them, and another to work as cash handler during some of the shifts. The owner was concerned with the hiring process, and she knew that whoever joined their food truck business would have to fit in with the three people who already knew each other fairly well.

I gave her some advice about being honest and open, along with posting a description for their job opening that captured the type of energy they wanted in their food truck. She followed my advice and decided to seek out a person who "had the patience of a yoga teacher who taught toddlers" and the adaptability of a "mother who worked from home" while also having a desire to "succeed in a unique culinary venture." There were other funny and witty lines as well. Ultimately, the people who applied for the job chose to apply in part because they thought the ad was humorous. When they hired their employees, they were able to find the energy they were looking for because they posted an ad that was honest about their requirements and told through their voice. The moral of this story is that this is *your* business. You will want to hire people who will stick around, whom you want to succeed with, and who have the same mission as you.

## In Conclusion

The hiring process may seem daunting, but it is only if you do not have this guidance. Now that I have given you these steps, you can move forward and discover what it is that you are looking for in your employees. Be honest about your needs and be willing to pay your employees for the skills they provide.

# HOW TO MARKET YOUR FOOD TRUCK BEFORE OPENING

*L*earning how to market is essential to your success as a food truck. Did you know that it is just as important to work on your marketing before you open? Most people don't know that you can actually begin building your community presence before opening day. There are a lot of ways you can start reaching your customers even before they have a chance to taste your food. It is important to do this so you can start building brand recognition, develop your food truck identity, and show people what they can expect before they begin visiting your food truck.

## COMMON MARKETING KNOWLEDGE You Should Know

I want to make it a point to go over some

marketing knowledge you should know as a food truck owner. There is a lot of information available to you as a new business online, but not all of the information regarding marketing will apply to you. Let's start by looking at what you should know about marketing as a food truck owner.

## MARKETING Is About Developing Relationships

Customers continue supporting businesses partially because they like the company. How many companies have you seen that have suffered large sales after they made an offensive choice, were rude towards customers, or made other decisions that impacted their likability? It happens more often now that we have social media to spread information rapidly; therefore, you need to start thinking of marketing as a way of building relationships with people. It's not always just about listening to your customers, or telling them what you want them to know—it's about maintaining a line of communication with them. Customers also want to see you giving back to your community. This does not necessarily mean that all of your profits need to be donated, but how do you, as a company, provide for the community you are a part of? What good deeds are you willing to do so your customers know you are a good person with a company they should support?

Networking is also important in developing a relationship. Some food truck owners make it a point to ask for customer names and learn the orders of their regular customers. Do you have a business you would visit each week? Can you do something that shows the employees are special to you because of their regular business? In addition to asking for their names, it is a good idea to introduce yourself as the owner. Even if you spend a lot of time cooking the meals, you will also want to take some time during each shift to give a quick hello to at least a few people. Be sure you also introduce yourself via social media and your company website.

## Sentimentality and Meaning Are Essential

Customers enjoy supporting companies that have a story behind them, and they want to get behind that story themselves too. Customers now have become more aware of how much buying power they have. In an age where many people make statements about what they do or do not support through their buying choices, people want to know why they should support you. An origin story gives them a little bit of that information; however, more than just an origin story, customers want to find meaning in all aspects of your business.

One good way to show they are valued is by creating a customer loyalty program, which many small businesses do through stamp cards. With stam cards, for each set amount of money or items a customer buys, they would receive a stamp. When the stamp card is filled, they can return with the card and receive a discount or free item. These are easy to produce and offer an incentive for returning customers. It isn't important just to bring in new customers—you also want to retain the customers you do get. You can build customer loyalty before you open by mailing out coupons, stamp cards, or giving coupons via social media or newspapers.

Customers like to see meaning in your menu. Why did you choose those items? Do you sell only items you love personally? You will want to make sure your employees have the same passion about your food that you do. How can you make your customers have this same perception? Before you open for business, you can use social media to share the importance of your menu items. Is one of your recipes a family recipe? Why not tell that story?

Be open and transparent about your costs and your menu items and list what you plan on selling on your website and social media before you open. Most of the time, if a customer knows how much they will spend when visiting your truck, they will be more likely to go, as they can fit it into their budget. It is better they know beforehand than for tem to show up and consider certain food overpriced.

. . .

**ONLINE PRESENCE IS 100% Necessary**

I've already given you some ideas for using your online presence before you open your business, but I wanted to focus on it completely in this section. Your online presence will likely be the first medium people on which people will start to notice your business. It is important that you make the most of every online interaction you can. Although your business will not operate primarily online, you will be interacting with customers online often because of the nature of your business. This might be done through frequent calendar updates, a changing menu, or tweets about new locations. By building and maintaining an online presence, you will be able to continue following trends. Social media will probably be how you conduct the majority of your business, and you will want to see what social media apps or websites your main demographics use; for example, Twitter would probably be more popular with some interests and age groups, whereas Facebook might be the choice for another demographic. It is a good idea to familiarize yourself with all of them, though you should ultimately focus on the one your customer base would be more likely to use. When you use social media, remember to use it as a business, as posting overly personal information that is unrelated to your business will likely cause you to lose followers. Aside from social media, your website will be the most used online source. Keep your website up-to-date and make sure it is user friendly. It is also a good idea to ensure your website can be easily navigated to by phone. Some websites choose to run a blog as well, where they would post extra tidbits of information, whether they be related to business growth, extra offerings, or discounts.

**ADVERTISEMENTS ARE a Great Way to Build Excitement For Your Business**

Before you open, you can begin building excitement for your food truck through advertisements; however, you need to be careful—advertising alone will not necessarily make people want to come to your business. How many bland commercials do you hear on the radio that don't invoke your interest? You should also think about what type of advertising would work best for your business and customer demographics, among a few other considerations to take as well.

· People do not read all the print ads. In general, most people only skim the headlines of an ad, so make sure your headlines count!

· In relation to audio ads, your customers would be reached much easier if they heard the ad multiple times, and success would be more likely if you were to launch a radio ad during a time when more potential customers are listening. An ad running at three in the morning is not likely to bring you as much business as an ad that plays for five days in a row during five o'clock traffic, for example.

· Direct mail advertising works best when there is an incentive. If you use direct mail advertising, be sure to include a coupon or a customer loyalty card.

Consider starting a YouTube channel which you can use for advertising your food truck. It is free and extremely effective. Companies like Nike and Adidas have used YouTube effectively to reach different markets without using as much as they normally would on traditional media.

**Tips on Marketing Before Opening Day**

Now that I've walked you through some of the most important elements and easy suggestions for marketing, I will start sharing some tips on how to market before your opening day.

1. **Develop your social media well before opening day and use it to promote your launch**. The best social media accounts are those that are active and engage with their customers. This means you cannot simply post things once a week; you should be posting daily—for Instagram, Pinterest, and Twitter—and twice a week for Facebook. Also, you need to be engaging with your customers by reading their responses to posts. If you are on Twitter, Facebook, or Instagram, you could like their posts as well. When you do post photos, share things

that customers might find interesting and give pictures of what you would be selling. You can also consider showing behind-the-scenes images and progress photos of your truck. Don't be afraid to follow the companies you like. Your goal with this piece of advice is essentially to be an engaged social media participant.

2. **Use giveaways as a way to boost interest**. Offer to give away a $30 gift card for people who like your Facebook page, then post about the give-away on other relevant Facebook pages (community events pages in your city for example). Offer a free sampler on opening day to the first five people in line and give away 50% off coupons to people who post about your new business. Find ways to offer a greater incentive for people to try out your business.

3. **Promote your business through local press**. You can offer sampler platters to local food writers before you open officially for business. If you can get food writers to talk about your business before it opens, you will see your business building a following pretty quickly. See if there are small business features for which you can be interviewed with local city magazines or newspapers.

4. **Create an email list and offer a 10% off coupon code to everyone who signs up for the email list before your opening day**. You can then use the email list to let everyone know where you will be during the first week of your business.

. . .

## In Conclusion

While many people believe marketing to be important after you open a business, how you market before opening will influence the success you have on opening day and beyond. Take advantage of the time you have to set yourself up for success, even before you open your food truck. Have a detailed marketing plan in place and follow through with it every step of the way. Take the information I have provided you in this chapter and adjust it to your business. Are there things you can think of that aren't here, but might work for your location and type of food truck? Don't be afraid to try them out!

# HOW TO PREPARE FOR
# OPENING DAY

*O*pening day is an exciting time for any food truck company. Now that you have learned how to market before your opening day, it is time to go over how to prepare for that opening day and what you can do to make it as successful as possible. I will discuss some marketing strategies, along with general tips to make the day, or time period, go well. Keep in mind that your opening day should be planned at least three months in advance.

## How to Make Opening Day Easier

Opening day will already be a stressful time because of the pressure you would probably be feeling to succeed. However, there are some things you can do to help make it run smoother.

1. **Opt for a simple menu**. While you might have plans to sell more items in the long run, you will want a simple menu during your grand opening. You and your employees will still be very new to cooking on demand and during a rush, so having a simple menu would be ideal. It would also make your costs lower in the beginning, as you will require fewer ingredients to buy. As you grow, your menu can also grow. You will want to make sure you set you and your employees up for success in every way possible. The first week of opening will also be a time when you will discover what works and what doesn't work —if you find that certain employees are unable to fill the role they were assigned to, it would probably be easier to work through that without the pressure of a large menu.

2. **Review all your paperwork before the official opening**. Go through all of your employees' forms and make sure everyone is set up for their first shift. Make sure to check your vendor agreements and double check work schedules, so you know you have coverage. Remember to look through your insurance information one more time —all your important paperwork should be stored in both your office and food truck, the latter in case you need to prove you are a business and your employees are authorized to work.

3. **Pick the big day!** Try to plan it during a time when you can be at a major event, like at a food

truck gathering or farmers market. You will want to do all you can to notify people about your opening in the two weeks prior to the actual day. Use social media during this time and consider doing a fun countdown giveaway or feature. Be sure to pick the day three months in advance and try to pair it with a city event.

4. **Consider doing a "soft opening" as well**. Pick your grand opening day, then have a soft opening a week or two before you actually open. In this case, you should only have a few staff members present and only allow some people to know about this opening. It will give you a chance to make sure the equipment is fully functioning, your people can work together in the truck, and you can easily maneuver it. A soft opening will help you identify any problems you may have, along with giving yourself time to adjust them.

5. **Invite the press to your grand opening**. This can include local food bloggers, local city newspapers, city magazines, or national food writers if you happen to be in the city a food writer lives in. See if you can get a feature on the local news. No matter which news medium you decide to advertise your food truck with, be sure to invite the press at least two weeks in advance.

6. **Keep in mind that a grand opening would probably last an entire week**. You might want to try to target specific customers on specific days of

your opening. For example, you can do a family friendly opening on a Saturday at a cultural event and have your grand opening near a club on a Friday night.

7. **Have someone focused on photos**. You will want to take as many photos as possible, but as we discussed during the chapter about employees, as the owner, you will have a lot on your plate. Therefore, you would probably want to assign this task to some of your employees. Have them take photos before, during, and after.

## How to Secure Local Press for Your Grand Opening

You might be able to get new customers through social media, but working with local press would give you a different kind of credibility and will help build buzz about your business much quicker. A good write-up from a food writer can serve as an unbiased review of your business' potential. It's important to get local press to your grand opening, but few people know exactly how to go about doing this. Here are a few ways you can get the local press involved with your grand opening:

1. **Host a tasting event**. It would be a good idea to do this after your soft opening, but maybe also before your grand opening. You can do it during the grand opening week too if you opt for a week

versus a day. Hosting a tasting event will give local writers and reporters an opportunity to taste your food and to discuss your business potential with other influencers. You, as the business, will also have a chance to speak to them in person and to tell them about your business, along with your story. While it may be hard to host an event the week of your opening, losing out on the profits and the time will guarantee that you have people who know about you and who are willing to share their experience with your business. A tasting event is also a controlled environment; if a food writer arrives on opening day and is stuck waiting in line, only to then wait longer for their food, they will be more likely to leave or be grouchy when they taste the food. A tasting event would guarantee a successful set up for their tasting.

2. **Use food holidays to your advantage**. If you are a waffle-focused company, for example, consider opening your food truck on National Waffle Day. There are numerous "food" holidays such as this for you to take advantage of. Aside from these holidays, if you have a cultural significance to your food, you can use a culturally relevant holiday to help boost your business. Cinco de Mayo weekend can be a great time to open a Mexican food truck. If you do this, you can easily partner with a local press or TV station to share a segment on the cultural significance of the holiday. You could even offer to do a

small cooking segment. Pitch about these events one to two months prior.

3. **Comp meals in exchange for the write up**. Do not do this for anyone who is a writer, but pick and choose who you most want to attend. If you do a tasting event, you can plan to comp everyone's meals; however, for the grand opening, be sure you get your writers and news anchors their food as soon as possible, then you comp them.

### Tips for a Successful Opening Day

I've given you some guidance in the two sections above, but there are still a lot of small tips and tricks I have to offer, which have been listed below. Take what sounds beneficial to you and feel free not to use what might not work for you. This is a collection of tips I have gathered over my years of giving business advice.

· **Hire enough workers and don't be afraid to overstaff your first few shifts**. The last thing you want is to be feeling overwhelmed during one of the most important times in your business. It might also be a good idea to have family help you out the first week, whether that be running social media, working the cash register, or keeping things clean.

· **Make a list of possible problems that might occur on your first day and do all you can to prepare for them in the event they do happen**.

Some examples might include the equipment not working, which you can avoid by checking your equipment before the opening week and the day before. Another issue might be that your staff called in sick. Can you avoid this by having an emergency employee be "on call" for opening week, just in case?

· **Focus on staying within your means**. While you might feel inclined to go all out and order t-shirts and tote bags to give away, only do this if it fits within your budget. At the end of the opening week, the amount of energy you dedicate to your work during the opening will make the most difference in your business potential—not how much free stuff you give away.

· **Consider what will be the best day to open your business**. Don't shoot to do it on the first of the month if it falls on a Wednesday. If you do decide to do it during a weekday, make sure you know *why* it is the best day. Weekends during large events tend to be best, but some people do well having a grand opening during a lunch shift in a business center. Find what works for your food truck.

· **Consider the season you decide to open your food truck**. If possible, aim for the summer, as that will be the best season for food truck businesses; however, September could also be a great month to open if you plan to sell near a local college or university. The season is equally as important as the weekday you choose to open on.

· **Try to take some notes**. If possible, consider carrying a voice recorder so you don't have to write them down. Opening day will test the systems you've put in place—you may learn that some things you've done work really well, whereas other choices maybe not so much. The notes you take will help you remember this without using up a lot of mental energy.

· **Motivate your team members**. Take the time to host a friendly informal gathering before the grand opening and have a team meeting to ask if anyone has any major concerns for the grand opening. Be open to receiving suggestions.

· **Invite everyone you know to the grand opening!** Don't worry about nerves or whether it is asking for too much support—just invite them! Ultimately, the people who want to support you will be there if it is possible, so it doesn't hurt to ask.

· Finally, **enjoy yourself!** It's a big day or a big week for you. You've worked really hard to get to opening day, so make the most of it.

### In Conclusion

Opening day is a big deal for you! It can be a stressful time for a lot of reasons, but there are also a lot of things you can do to prepare for it and make it easier on yourself. Follow the list of tips I provided above to help bring in press and make the event the most successful it can be. But above all else, enjoy yourself and be proud of all the work you've put into it.

# HOW TO MARKET AFTER YOUR TRUCK OPENS

*M*uch of the marketing advice I have already covered is about building up the energy and excitement for opening your food truck. This chapter will now focus on how to continue marketing your food truck and ways you can maintain the excitement from your grand opening permanently. Marketing is essential for continuing to build your customer base and keeping current customers interested.

## USING Business Marketing to Your Advantage

There are many traditional ways of marketing that can be used to market your food truck business. I will be going over a few of the best ways to use business marketing as a tool.

· · ·

## SHARE YOUR MESSAGE

Remember that "key word" or main "message" we discussed earlier? Once your food truck is running, you'll want to continue sharing that message with potential customers. Some people choose to do this by printing copies of their menu and handing them out. This can be done at county fairs, local cultural events, or even while out at the park. You can opt to send them as direct mail marketing as well. Some food trucks send postcards with coupon codes, which are affordable, easy to produce, and can be mailed for a small cost. You'll want to find as many ways as possible to reach your customer base frequently. Many food trucks use email lists to keep their customers updated, and you can even ask if people want to sign up for a list when they make a purchase.

## WORK ON YOUR **Reputation**

It's important to create and maintain a good reputation for your business. Once you are open, you will want to find ways to create a high reputation for yourself. Make sure you are consistently practicing quality control, as your food should be just as good on day 100 as it was on opening day. Once returning customers realize they can trust your menu and food to be consistently high-quality, you can guarantee they will be likely to rave about your food truck to people they know. It is also a good idea to consider how you can make a positive impact on your community. A company can earn a positive reputation by making smart choices, such as donating extra food to the local homeless population, working with local farms, or offering discounts to respected community members (teachers for example).

### HANDLE COMPETITION with Grace

It is very likely there will be other food trucks in your area who are competing for space and customers. It is also likely that there will be other food trucks with your type of cuisine, unless you have something absolutely unique. Even with a similar menu, you should never resort to berating or putting down other companies. Chances are, they went through a very similar situation as you did in starting their business. Use your business marketing skills to promote your food truck, but don't resort to negativity as a way to stand out.

### DEVELOP a Marketing Budget

Marketing is important in helping you become successful, but it also comes with a cost. Some forms of marketing may be affordable, but others may cost more. If you end up hiring someone to run your social media accounts, that would be an additional cost that you need to account for. The best way to ensure you are marketing actively without taking money from other expenses is by creating a marketing budget, and it is generally recommended that you aim for about 2-5% of your total sales as part of your marketing budget. The more money you make, the more you can spend. As you use your marketing budget, aim for a variety of marketing techniques. If radio ads work for you, feel free to use them more than once, but don't rely solely on one method to gain new customers.

**Ways to Promote Your Food Truck**

Now that I have introduced you to methods that apply to all small businesses, I want to give you more tips on how to promote your food truck, pull in new customers, and expand your reach. Keep in mind that current customers also have the potential to bring in new sales by becoming repeat customers; therefore, you should also include reaching out to those familiar to your truck one of your food truck marketing strategies.

· **Reach out to local organizations**. You can reach out to local unions, political organizations, community clubs, or even business-related organizations. Try to collect potential phone numbers or email addresses early in your business career and reach out to one or two a month.

· **Expand your friendship circle**. If you are part of a big city, get to know people who interact with tourists often. Travel agencies or local foodies are a great place to start. You can even give your information to local convention centers, the concierge staff of big hotels, vacation rental offices, and even gas stations. The more menus you share, the more likely people will come across one.

· **Reach out to different companies**. Some large companies in your area may be in need of catering services, and it's always a good idea to give your information to both small and large business owners. If they have your prices for large orders and your menu, they will be more likely to reach out to you than try to find a new restaurant to order from. Be sure to also give them details about how soon they need to order and what would be involved in a rush order.

· **Decide to check in with current customers**. This is something you can do both during and after your shifts. Once you handle the majority of orders, go ask how the food is and make sure your customers are happy. If someone is not happy, fix the issue immediately. Thank your customers for giving you their business. If you have customers fill out customer experience cards, personally thank those who share their information with you, and if there are any issues with their experience, apologize and see if there are ways you can fix it.

· **Stay up to date on local events**. Follow community calendars, watch out for library events, and know when farmers markets and swap meets are happening. If you decide not to have the truck open at those events, you can still attend and hand out your menu to people who might be interested.

· **Remember to be kind and nice, not demanding**. Don't expect customers to go to your food truck, get angry if they don't want a copy of your menu, or be rude to customers who complain. All of this should be obvious advice.

### Low-Cost Marketing

For those of you who don't make large profits early on, it might be a good idea to scale back on the marketing budget. Thankfully, there are still ways to market your business while also keeping it at a low cost. Here are a few budget-friendly ways to market:

1. **Consider starting a blog on your website**. Definitely start a website if you don't have one, as blogs are an excellent, low-cost way to keep your followers up-to-date on what is happening with your food truck. If you want to gain more readers, you might also consider adding other free and engaging content, such as recipes, how-to videos, giveaways, and even behind-the-scenes videos.

2. **Offer to be a guest blogger**. There are multiple food truck blogs, restaurant blogs, and local food writers who are always looking for new ways to add engaging content to their mediums. If you offer to be a guest blogger, you would be giving them free content to use in exchange for allowing you to link your website and give a short description of your food truck and company. If you don't mind writing, this is one way to find new customers and build a connection with a local writer. Often, if you guest blog for someone else, they might also be willing to guest blog for you.

3. **Offer returning customer incentives, like loyalty cards or coupons, for their next visit**. You can ask for a short survey in exchange or simply hand it out with a receipt. Offering a discount on the next purchase might make the customer more likely to come back. Once they have returned two or three times, they will be more likely to return more often.

4. **Offer first-time customer discounts**. You can do this through email, a website, or even deal websites like Groupon. This is a great way to make it easier for a customer to be willing to try your food truck instead of a place they are familiar with.

5. **Offer cooking classes**. During these courses, you can show your customers how to prepare a simple dish from your menu. You can host it in a local community center or ask an apartment complex if they would like to host it in a clubhouse.

If you do this, you can gain new customers while also showing off your (or your chef's) culinary skills.

6. **Rely on the exposure of social media**. Make it a point to use social media often if you do not have a marketing budget. The more you engage, the more people will follow you or engage with your content. If you have 10 followers and only 1 person tries out your restaurant, that is a 10% chance of bringing in a new customer. If you have 100 customers and you bring in 10%, that is 10 people. The more followers, the greater your chances of bringing in new customers.

## In Conclusion

There are a variety of ways to market your food truck once you are open, and the important thing is that you continue improving your marketing strategies and building a marketing budget. While you may not have outstanding profits early on, there are still many affordable ways for you to reach new customers and retain your old ones. Not every method will work for you, but it is a good idea to try something first before you decide it will not work.

# HOW TO TURN A PROFIT

*N*ow that you know how to bring in new customers and encourage repeat customers, I will now be focusing on the next important element in your business: turning a profit. Once you actually have your food truck up and running, your main focus should be finding ways to increase your profit, so you can pay back any outstanding debts and provide a good living for yourself. This chapter will focus on managing food and inventory costs, creating quality customer experiences, and other suggestions for boosting your profits.

## LOWERING FOOD COSTS

As I mentioned in the chapter about food pricing, managing your food costs and pricing your menu will be large parts of how slowly or quickly you turn a profit. This is why it will be my first focus point in this chapter. We've already discussed menu pricing, so as a quick reminder, you need to price according to ingredients, added value, and preparation costs to ensure you don't lose money on your menu. Outside of menu pricing, however, you can make a greater profit by reducing the amount of money you spend on your ingredients. You have some options when it comes time for shopping that will help reduce your costs. Don't sacrifice quality, but be wise with how you spend your money.

· **Try out warehouses or bulk shops**. Many of these stores offer greater prices on products by selling large amounts of them. It isn't only for paper goods and frozen food however; there are many warehouses that offer great quality meats for a good cost. Many also sell fresh produce in bulk. If you do decide to buy in bulk, be sure you have adequate storage space for your food items, so they remain fresh. Also, remember to check the sell-by date when you shop. These stores are a great option for paper goods, cleaning supplies, and even trash bags. A membership is usually a small fee that pays itself off with only a few shopping trips. Stores like Costco and Sam's Club offer business membership cards which can help you keep your business expenses separate from your personal expenses.

Grow your own vegetable supply in the garden in

your backyard. The supply may not be sufficient to provide for all your needs in the food truck but you can supplement what you are already purchasing and bring down your costs.

· **Shop sales at your local grocery stores**. While they don't always have the best prices, you can often sign up for email coupons or use the weekly ad coupons. When you shop wisely, you can wind up getting free items or a great deal on expensive ingredients. If you are in an area that allows you to stack coupons, you could wind up saving even more.

· **Local farms and farmers market**: If you offer local ingredients or organic produce, you will want to shop with local farmers or at a farmers market. Depending on how much you buy of certain produce, you might be able to strike a deal with a farmer. By shopping through local farms, you will also be able to feature seasonal items and offer a revolving, seasonal menu. Consistently working with the same local farm will likely give you lower costs for great quality, and it will help you build a local relationship.

· **Specialty shops**. If you sell a specific cuisine, or use unique ingredients that are only found at select specialty shops, you might want to consider developing a relationship with the owner. If they know you will be buying certain items often, they may be able to offer you a better price. Don't be afraid to ask, but always begin by introducing yourself.

. . .

### LEARN TO REDUCE Waste

Food waste is a growing epidemic, but not only is it harmful on a large scale, but it is also harmful to your business. The restaurant industry tends to throw away up to 10% of its food inventory, even before it is used. Add in food that is mishandled, wasted, or improperly cooked, and that number ends up getting even higher. Cutting back on food waste is one way to lower your food costs, so take advantage of daily specials to sell items that are at risk of going bad. Find ways to use products that might not be as visually appealing. Many food trucks prepare their own vegetable or meat stock with scraps; not only does this cut down on waste, but it also saves you from spending more money on an ingredient. You might also consider pickling certain foods that are nearing their sell-by date. Be sure to enforce quality standards by ensuring each meal is prepared the same way. Create menu specials or one-day features to upsell an ingredient. Stay up-to-date on inventory and don't order things out of habit; only get what you need before the next purchase.

### KEEP YOUR CUSTOMERS Happy

Reducing food waste and costs is one way to

easily increase your profits, but beyond that, keeping the customer happy will also lead to return business. Here are some small strategies you can use to keep your customers happy, so they will recommend your food truck and return for more meals.

1. **Treat every meal like it's your grand opening meal**. By this, I mean you should take the same care and caution each shift that you did on your very first shift. The customer should be getting great and consistent quality food that tastes similar to the last time they ate it. While you do want a quick speed, do not sacrifice the quality of the food just to serve more people. It is better that you serve a good quality meal in an average wait time than to serve many mediocre meals at a rapid pace.

2. **Do more than just cook the food or take the order**. Actively engage with your customers at every shift by getting to know them by name and asking them how their day is going. You might not be able to do this the entirety of the shift, but you can do so during a slow period, or after a rush. Providing good customer service will lead to more returning customers.

3. **Be open to learning**. This is especially true when you run into customer complaints. Some customers will likely be wrong, but there will be many more who are right; therefore, do not assume you know everything. If a customer is unhappy do what you can to make them happy. If you cannot do

so, then thank them for their business and move on. Even with amazing food, you will not stay in business if you cannot keep your customers happy, so aim to do your best with every shift. Be willing to learn and adjust when you need to improve something. If you find multiple people complaining about a food item, reconsider that recipe. You don't need to change everything, but keep an open mind if the issue seems to occur often.

### Tips to Increase Your Profits

Food costs and customer retention will be your biggest profit boosters, but there are many other small changes you can make and habits to instill that can help you save money overall, thus increasing your profits. Here is a list of some easy-to-follow tips that will boost your profits.

· **Stay up to date on your operational costs**. You should know exactly how much it costs to keep your business afloat and sell certain menu items. By frequently checking in with your costs and sales, you can make changes where they are needed (like cutting a menu item that is eating your profits instead of adding to them).

· **Learn to value your time**. This begins with delegating tasks that can be done easily by someone else. As the owner, you will have a lot to manage; if you are also the chef or a cook, you will be even busier trying to keep your food standards high and your business running. Don't be afraid to delegate time-consuming tasks. This is why I had an entire chapter on hiring good employees. Once you hire good employees, you can then trust them with tasks, allowing you to focus on more important aspects of your business.

· **Make sure the people who work the windows and cash register are friendly and happy staff members**. They should be accustomed to making small talk, be comfortable introducing themselves, willing to answer questions, and do it all with a smile. If your customers feel like a bother to the window staff, there is a higher chance they will not return. Beyond that, if a customer can't get a clear answer on ingredients and are worried about allergies, they won't return. Your staff members should be focused, knowledgeable, and able to move quickly, but they should also do it while making the customer feel like a priority.

· **Learn to understand customers' wants**. While you might love a certain menu item, if people aren't buying it, it will only cost your business more money to keep selling it. Learn to evaluate what is doing well and what isn't working, so you can keep your customers happy.

· **Offer catering services**. Once you have a handle on selling from your food truck, catering should be an easy way to add a big income boost.

You can do it while still maintaining other calendar commitments, and it is a good way to promote your business. Weddings are prime events where a food truck can offer catering services. For example, a wedding with 150 guests can bring in a profit of $3,000 to $6,000.

## In Conclusion

The two biggest ways to improve your profit margin is by reducing food costs and keeping current customers happy. Reducing your food costs can be done in many different ways, whether it is through reduction of food waste or lowering ingredient costs. You may not be able to make every customer happy, but you should aim to please most of them. Part of keeping a steady business is growing your customer retention.

# HOW TO SCALE IN YOUR FIRST YEAR

$\mathcal{I}$f your food truck does well in its first year, you might want to consider scaling. For those who are unaware, scaling means expanding your business. Some people might be interested in opening a second food truck, whereas others might want to expand to a brick and mortar restaurant. I will talk about both of those options in the next two chapters. For this chapter, I will focus on the dos and don'ts of expanding, how to expand your business, and introduce you to an easy way to grow your business: a mall kiosk. These are all easy things that can be done in your first year of business.

## HOW TO SUCCESSFULLY Grow Your Business
· **Get to know every job on your food truck**. You should, as the owner, be able to pick up the

slack wherever there is some. Even if you hire other employees, it is important that you know how to fill any role. By doing this, you will know what to look for in future employees as you expand your business. This will also help you learn to pay attention to detail in each job role.

Utilize your social following. If you already have a social following that you have built up over the years why not use it to build a loyal customer base. Those who have eaten from your previous establishment will definitely patron your new place and by word of mouth let others know about it.

· **Be passionate about what you're doing.** You will never expand if you hate working on your food truck. Show your vendors that you enjoy working with them and value the products they provide. Make sure your customers know you love your business and value them supporting you. You will not be able to get investors in the future, nor will you be able to raise a profit, without enthusiasm.

· **Always keep your focus on the customer.** Do this, even if it means sacrificing some small aspects of what you hoped your business would be. Don't change the entirety of your food truck for one customer, but if many customers complain about a certain taste or a quality of your food truck, consider changing it. You will ultimately need the customer if you want to stay in business.

· **Be competitive, but in a good way.** This means

working on finding new food truck locations to boost your sales. See what other food truck companies do well and how you can do it better. You should also improve your social media following and aim for more followers than other local trucks, while always trying to be better today than you were yesterday.

· **Fully understand your money**. You will not be able to gain new investors and grow your business if you do not understand your own finances. Likewise, you won't be able to decide what course of action to take within your first year if you don't know how to improve your profit margin. Always work on ways to improve your profits.

· **Aim to do your best every day**. You want to try to achieve excellence in every dish, interaction, and event.

· **Learn to set goals and achieve them**. This can be in the form of daily, weekly, monthly, and quarterly sales goals. You can also try to set goals for selling a certain number of dishes, discovering a new number of locations, or improving your email subscriber list. Setting goals and giving yourself small deadlines will help you improve continuously.

## The Dos and Don'ts of Growing Your Food Truck Business

**<u>Do</u> take the time to familiarize yourself with information about how you want to expand**. If you want to open a new brick and mortar restaurant, research the differences in running a restaurant versus running a food truck and see if there is a market for your type of cuisine in the local area. You might want to hire certain specialists, such as an accountant or an attorney, when you go through this process. Both of these people can help you organize your finances and decide if expansion is feasible. An attorney can give you guidance on the differences regarding the legality of your plan.

**DON'T RUSH to expand so fast that you are no longer able to manage what you started with**. Growing your business quickly will always put a lot of pressure on you and on your employees. Expanding will require as much attention as you gave when you first started your food truck, so only expand once you can trust that your employees are able to manage the food truck with you gone more often.

**<u>Do</u> FIND new financing options for your expansion**. Once you have already proven yourself successful as a food truck owner, you will have a new credibility that will help you gain investments. You might also qualify for other small business loans. If your food truck is doing well, don't put it up as collateral unless that becomes the only option. If your second business does not go as planned, you don't want to lose the one that is doing well too.

Don't let **your standards dip**. As I mentioned earlier, if you expand, your attention will probably be turned to focus on the expansion of your business and less on your current food truck. You need to find other ways to make sure your quality does not suffer and that your customers do not have negative experiences because you are unable to be there for every shift. Keep your standards high, and hire a manager who will also maintain them.

Do be **realistic about your expansion**. Just like how your food truck needed time to turn a larger profit, your new business will likely need even *more* time. You might want to open multiple food trucks or many restaurants, but you need to be honest about how quickly that can actually happen. Trying to open more than one food truck at a time is a recipe for disaster, so don't put your entire business at risk because you are greedy about the speed at which you want your business to grow.

.  .  .

DON'T CONFLATE **the two markets**. If you are opening a brick and mortar restaurant, the needs will be drastically different from your food truck. Just because you do well in one does not mean you will automatically do well in the other. How you reach customers will need to change, your menu items might have to shift, and your customer experience will also need to be addressed. The entirety of your brand and identity may stay the same, but different markets all have different needs.

## Is a Mall Kiosk a Good Expansion Idea in Your First Year?

If you believe you are ready to expand in your first year but you want to jump right into a full-scale restaurant, you could consider having a mall kiosk. While mall profits have dipped due to online sales, many malls are still doing well—food courts in the mall especially so. People enjoy the experience of going to a mall, even if they don't make all their purchases there. Therefore, a mall kiosk could be a great way to expand your business and test your potential for a full-scale restaurant.

A mall kiosk can provide a great deal of foot traffic, as people who go to a mall often have a meal while they are visiting many of the shops within.

You will be more likely to gain foot traffic customers in a mall than in a freestanding restaurant. Also, a mall offers a controlled environment—the heating, cooling, hours, and lighting are all controlled by the mall. You will not need to open as many accounts as you would if you were starting your own business. Unlike a food truck, you can remain open even during the rainy season, and you don't need to shut down because an event ended early. Most malls cause you to set standard hours, which means you can have more predictable shifts than you would in a food truck. There is also the bonus of mall security during off hours.

While you will have to pay a rent fee that typically includes utilities, cleaning, and other services only given to people who have shops inside a mall, you can still often get discounts at other mall shops and restaurants as well. With a mall kiosk, you can learn how to manage having a physical, constant location and use it as an opportunity to practice what you are learning about physical restaurants.

## In Conclusion

Expansion is a great idea to think about, even early on. If you are thinking about scaling in your first year, make sure you are not jumping too far ahead or trying to manage too much. A good option for expansion during your first year is to open a mall kiosk, which can be a good way to "practice" if you are thinking about opening a brick and mortar restaurant down the line.

# HOW TO SCALE IN YEAR 2-5

*W*hile some of you might be ready to start scaling your business in the first year you are open as a food truck, many more of you will feel ready in year two through five of being in business. Some things are good to do sooner but expanding your business should take time. You are more likely to succeed if you allow yourself to get settled in your current business and choose to expand after you have stabilized your food truck. In this chapter, we will focus on scaling your food truck business by expanding to a brick and mortar restaurant. I'll explain some of the key differences in opening a brick and mortar restaurant, along with giving you guidance on where to begin your search.

. . .

## SHOULD I Expand Into a Brick and Mortar Restaurant?

Many people who choose to open a food truck business choose to do so because they have an interest in starting their own culinary business while avoiding the big startup cost requirements of a full-scale restaurant. Food trucks are easier to manage and don't require as much startup, and if you also chose to start a food truck for the same reason, there will come a point when you may become interested in swapping to a brick and mortar restaurant.

Some of the starting points will be the same as they were for your food truck. You'll need to find a solid funding source. You will also have to know a lot about your brand and your projected profits, along with other aspects of your business plan. You will need to do market research and find a quality location. Beyond that, make note of some differences between the two businesses. Your location cannot change, and you can't experiment as much as you can with your food truck. You will need to invest in more equipment, supplies, food, and staff; however, it is entirely possible and often a good move to make.

You need to know what it is you want to do with your restaurant. Why are you looking to expand? What can a full-scale restaurant do that your food truck cannot do? In what ways will expanding benefit your business? Knowing the answers to these questions will help you make the best decision about the size of your expansion and seek the right level of funding. You will also want to decide if you will name your restaurant the same as your food truck. Many people do this, though others choose to do a variation of the same name.

### Three Things You Need to Establish

If you are choosing to expand your food truck into a brick and mortar restaurant, there are three things you should decide: your brand, desired location (general idea is fine), and how you plan to operate your business. We will look more closely at each of these.

1. **Brand**. By now, you should have worked to establish your brand. Your food truck was your "experiment" and will provide you with quality information about how well-received your "brand" has been. While you may make changes in the atmosphere, menu, and staff, the changes should not be drastic. In general, your brick and mortar restaurant should have the same emotion or essence as your food truck. The atmosphere of your brick and mortar restaurant should not change drastically from your

food truck, as you would likely want to bring in both new and repeat customers.

2. **General location**: With a food truck, you are able to work some shifts in certain areas, move if the weather is not great, and show up at events with built-in crowds; with a brick and mortar restaurant, you will not have these options. Location is much more important at this step of your business than it was initially. If you have been open for two to five years already, you probably know by this point what parts of the city will work well and have your customer demographics. Use this knowledge to your advantage. Don't opt for an unknown location; establish your full-scale restaurant in an area where you know it has a better chance of succeeding.

3. **How you plan to operate**. With a food truck, you had fewer employees working in the food truck and likely had select roles to fill. When you move to a brick and mortar restaurant, it will require more employees, tasks will need to be further separated, and you'll be managing multiple customers at once. This can be even more complicated when you're running both a food truck and a restaurant. If you have excess food on the food truck, will you be selling it in the restaurant or will they be completely separate? Will your restaurant also serve as the commercial kitchen for your food truck? You need to sort out exactly how your businesses will work

with each other. While they may be two separate entities, they are both yours and of the same brand.

## A Quick Story...

I once consulted with an owner who was looking to expand from a food truck to a brick and mortar restaurant. She was having difficulty getting investors for her new venture, despite having a successful food truck. We sat down and went over her business plan, which was detailed and showed great potential for success; however, it was once I went through her business plan that I found the problem. People were hesitant to invest because she was trying to open an upscale brick and mortar restaurant when her food truck had been more casual, homestyle cooking. In the owner's mind, the next step was to move to an upscale restaurant. Investors did not know whether it would succeed because it was so different from her food truck, even if the recipes were based on similar ideas. I explained to her that she did not need to jump to an upscale status to succeed or expand. Once I explained that her business could remain quite similar to the food truck, she was finally able to see the potential in her own project. After reframing her business plan, she was able to secure an investment.

. . .

ONCE YOU DECIDE **to Expand**

There are some things you can do to help ensure your full-scale restaurant's success.

1. **Once you have your location bought or leased, invest in a high-quality sign**. The sign needs to be visible, legible, and will last a while. The sign is also the very impression your customers will get of your restaurant. Feel free to use a similar style to your food truck logo and design, but a slight change can also benefit it. If you plan to have your brick and mortar restaurant differ from your food truck slightly, the sign is a good way to let customers know to expect this.

2. **Make your menu easy to read and understand, just like you would for your food truck**. Thankfully, you also know what has been successful on your food truck. Instead of opting for an entirely new menu, add items that you know are good sellers. With these items, you can include new ones as well; however, don't overfill the menu. Keep it simple by offering only a small number of entrées (no more than ten). Just like you did with your food truck's grand opening, keep the menu simple and easy-to-manage for your kitchen staff. Once they succeed, you can either rotate seasonal menu items or include a few more options.

3. **Know what people are looking for in a**

**restaurant**. While you will bring some food truck customers to your restaurant, you will also be trying to reach a slightly different demographic or, at the very least, entice your customers with a new experience. Feel free to ask your customers what they expect when they go to a restaurant. Find out what kind of atmosphere your ideal customers prefer in regard to color, lighting, and sound, as well as how much the furniture affects whether they try a new restaurant. Use every opportunity you can to learn new information about your market.

4. **Stick with your brand**. Do not change it drastically or opt for an entirely new kind of experience. Stick with what you know and what has been successful.

**In Conclusion**

Scaling your food truck in years two through five is a great choice! If you are someone who opened a food truck to work toward a full-scale restaurant, then know it is an entirely reasonable possibility. Opening a successful brick and mortar restaurant will require more time, energy, and resources, but it is often worth it if you make the right choices.

**GET Your $397 Bonuses With This Link- https://bit.ly/2IlMu6l**

- Tax And Accounting Templates**($17 Value)**
- Bookkeeping Basics Tutorial Video**($47 Value)**
- Video Reveals  How To Save Hundreds Of Dollars With A Tax Firm **($63 Value)**
- Updates When New Food Truck Strategies Are Discovered!**($200 Value)**

# SEVEN MISTAKES FOOD TRUCKS MAKE AND HOW TO AVOID THEM

*C*hapters one through fourteen have mainly given you advice about how to find success as a food truck owner. Now that we are nearing the end of the book, I wanted to dedicate a short chapter to common mistakes many food truck owners make. I hope that by sharing these mistakes and giving you advice for avoiding them, you can learn from them. I'm not saying you won't make mistakes, but by learning from others, you can hopefully avoid and make fewer mistakes than other new food truck businesses.

1. **Not being prepared**. By reading this book, you will already know more and be ahead of most new food truck owners. While I may be able to give you a lot of handy information, there will still be a lot you

need to do to prepare yourself for your new business. Many new food truck owners make the mistake of "just winging it" or trying to learn as they go. Do not fall into this trap—take the time to study other successful food trucks and read books such as this one. Also, prepare yourself financially. The first three months will be the most difficult months for you, so don't jump into your food truck venture without enough savings to keep yourself afloat. If you need to have family help you for staff or lodging during this time, do so.

2. **Having a grand opening that flops**. Your grand opening will be what sets you up for success, so be sure to take the time to plan a successful event. There may be some issues, but if you take the time to prepare and plan out for worst-case scenarios, you will already be way ahead most people who just picked a random day to open for business. Do what you can to promote the event and pick a time and day that will be the most likely to bring you new customers. Also, consider doing a soft opening to help alleviate some pressure.

3. **Trying to expand too quickly**. Remember what we discussed earlier? When you start expanding your business, your initial food truck will lose some of your attention. If your food truck is still in a vulnerable state (the first six months to a year), it can suffer easily because you were too focused on expanding. Let your business grow organically and

don't rush yourself too soon. You will be much more likely to make greater profits by waiting to expand in year three versus rushing and growing in month six.

4. **Never creating a true identity or brand**. Many people think the name and the cuisine will do all the work for them, but that is not the case. You need to go through the chapter on branding and figure out exactly what it is that makes your food truck unique. Decide on the emotions you want to convey the most and don't make the mistake of expecting your designs and menu to do all the story-telling.

5. **Not having a strong social media presence**. A food truck will need a heavy social media presence to be successful. Unlike a brick and mortar restaurant, the locations and menu are ever revolving with a food truck, and social media will keep your customers updated about both. So many food trucks fail to reach their true potential in their first year because they didn't see social media as important. Even if you do not personally like social media, that does not mean it won't be beneficial for your business because it's an easy way to reach people. Beyond just creating an account, you will need to keep it updated. Many food trucks make the mistake of opening accounts and never updating it or engaging with their followers, or failing to grow

their following. Work on social media like you would your business plan.

6. **Doubting yourself**. It is easy to think you cannot do what you are doing, especially in the early stages. Many people also worry they will "fail." The truth is, if you are reading this book, you are already moving toward starting a business. By taking this step, you are already doing what thousands of people wish they could do: work toward starting a business. If you buy your food truck, you're doing even more, and if you set a date for a grand opening, you have done more than millions of people will ever do in their lifetime. Therefore, be proud of the work you are doing, understand that you will make mistakes and learn from them, and trust that you have the potential to follow through and succeed. Doubting yourself only takes time away from more important matters. On the other hand, do not become so over-confident that you do not put in the work. The truth is, a tiny bit of doubt is good because it pushes you to succeed; in excess, however, it can be harmful.

7. **Trying to do everything**. So many food truck owners think they can be the accountant, chef, social media person, and manager all at once. Trying to do this will only lead you to failure. You cannot manage absolutely everything and if you try, you will wind up only giving partial attention to the task at hand because you're too busy thinking about what you

have to tweet later that day. Do not be afraid to dele-gate. This is why you hire quality employees so you can trust them with tasks. If you need to, ask family to join you in the early stages. If you have close friends whom you trust, then ask them to join as well. The key is to surround yourself with people you trust so you can feel comfortable asking them to handle parts of the operation.

# HOW TO ABIDE BY THE LAW

*T*his chapter is the closing chapter because it is important to know but will be something you will also have to research on your own. In this chapter, I will go over some basic food truck regulations you must abide by, give you basic accounting information, share details about taxes, and talk about food regulations. You may or may not be familiar with these topics, but by the end of the chapter, you should have a general knowledge about all of them. It will still be your responsibility to research what applies in your city, as well as if there are any additional regulations you must follow.

## Food Truck Licenses **and Permits**

To operate your food truck, you will be required to have certain licenses and permits in your truck at all times. You will need them before you can begin selling, and make note that they will vary by city, county, and by state.

1. **Your Employer Identification Number (EIN)**. This is required by the IRS and identifies your food truck as a business. It is used for tax purposes and as a way to hire employees. You can apply for this number for free through the IRS website, or by mail and fax.

2. **Business license**. You need this in order to operate. You may be charged a yearly fee to continue having this license, which might be a percentage of sales or a flat fee. Laws related to your business license can change often; therefore, you will want to be added to a mailing list for your county and city laws, so you don't accidentally break a regulation.

3. **Your license for your vehicle**. You need to make sure the driver and vehicle are both allowed to drive. The requirements will vary depending on the size of the vehicle, and some states will require certain-sized food trucks to have a commercial license. In that case, only drivers with a commercial license will be allowed to drive the vehicle.

4. **A permit to sell**. This is required in some states and will come with a small fee at the time of application. It does, however, also give you the right to buy some items at a wholesale cost.

5. **Permit to handle food**. This is required in some cities and states by the employees of the food

truck. In basic terms, this permit states that the employee has been trained in food handling safety. Be sure you require your employees to have this training, whether your city requires it or not. It is better to have it.

6. **A permit from the health department**. You will be required to be routinely inspected by your local health department, just as any restaurant would. They will make sure you are following safety protocol.

7. **Fire certificate**. The fire department will want to make sure your food truck is ready to run and the equipment does not pose a dangerous threat to you, your employees, or your customers. There will likely be routine inspections.

## Accounting Basics

I highly recommend hiring an accountant your first year in business until you fully understand all that is required in managing your financial records. However, in the event that you didn't do this early on, I wanted to share some basic accounting information. Here are some things of which you should consistently know, keep track, and be aware.

1. **Cash flow**. You should know exactly where your money is going and how much money is coming in. It is a consistent game of balancing your budgets and making sure you are spending less than

you're making. If you don't already budget in your personal life, that is a good way to become familiar with cash flow in businesses.

2. **Record keeping**: You need to be recording all of your income actively, along with all of your expenses; however, you should not be mixing your personal expenses with your business expenses. Come tax time, things will go much smoother if you have clear records of all relevant transactions. Don't collect all your receipts in a box, but be sure you have things categorized and organized. Most point-of-sale (POS) systems will track all your income for you, and some even track how much is spent on ingredients; nevertheless, you will still need to manage this in another format.

It is a good idea to set up a business checking account. This type of account is also known as the demand account. They are liquid and accessed using cheques making it easy to track you expenditures away from personal purchases.

3. **Inventory**. Your business will rely on you having the right amount of inventory at all times. Too much of one thing could mean spending a lot on food waste and having suffering sales. Consider your inventory as another type of cash—you need to track it, know where it is going, and where you are wasting it.

4. **Profit and loss statement**. This is a summary of all of your income, expenses, and inventory, while

showing you your total loss and profits. These should definitely be done quarterly, but it is best if you can do them monthly and weekly, especially early in your business. It will make it easier to form sales goals, track cash flow, and budget.

5. **Software**. There are many different software systems you can turn to as a means of managing your accounting information. You can also opt to take a community college accounting course. It is a good idea to get a POS system that can help make some of these tasks easier for you. Many newer POS systems can create reports or track inventory automatically for you.

### Taxes: **The Basics**

While I won't be able to give you all the information you need about taxes, I am hoping to give you a basic understanding that you can build on. First, what business entity you use will determine how you deal with income tax. Let's look at these main business entities:

1. **Sole proprietorship**. Many new businesses start with a sole proprietorship until they make a larger profit. It is the easiest to create and the most affordable option; however, it does come with some issues, mainly that your business will not be protected legally. If you face any legal issues, your personal assets will also suffer. In regard to taxes,

you don't have to file paperwork that deals with incorporation—you would simply file your personal 1040 yearly, and you would add on "profit and loss" from business, along with a self-employment tax. As you make a larger profit, you may be required to file more often or pay a certain amount of taxes in intervals instead of yearly. This usually happens if you're expected to pay more than $1,000 in taxes yearly.

2. **LLC or Limited Liability Company**. These are good options for small businesses. They offer some legal protection while only costing a percentage of what S or C corporations cost. They are also not as difficult to manage. The fee is greater than the previous option, though the main benefit would be that an LLC protects your personal assets from being affected by business losses. Tax filing will be similar to the sole proprietorship, in that you file an SE form along with your 1040 income tax form. You will be liable to pay quarterly taxes, depending on how much you are expected to pay.

3. **Partnership**. A partnership is a good option if there is more than one party involved. They can range in complexity from resembling a sole proprietorship to being set up similarly to an LLC. You and your partner would decide how the partnership is set up, whether that be all profits and losses split evenly or in a different fraction. Taxes can be complicated when it comes to a partnership because you're dealing with two people.

. . .

**In Conclusion**

With the above information, you now have an introduction into licensure, taxes, and accounting that you will need to navigate as a food truck business owner. The best thing you can do is speak to a professional early on to help navigate all of this information. You do not need to hire a full-time accountant to start, but it might be wise to pay to speak to one for a few hours, so they can help you make the right choice for your business. There is plenty of information online and at your local library if you are determined to handle it on your own early on.

# AFTERWORD

Well done! You have reached the end of this book. By now, you should have a detailed idea of how to start your own food truck business. In this book, we covered topics such as drafting a business plan, choosing a location, narrowing down customer demographics, and even discussed all the ways marketing will benefit you, all in great detail. Even if you knew nothing about business before this, with this book, you now know what it takes to create a successful food truck business.

With this newfound knowledge, it is now up to you to move forward and begin taking the necessary steps toward creating your food truck business. With the many tips I've provided, you now have first-hand knowledge of what it takes to be successful in this market. With this book, I believe you have the potential to start a strong food truck business. More importantly however, do you believe you can do it?

**Get Your $397 Bonuses With This Link- https://bit.ly/2IlMu6l**

- Tax And Accounting Templates**($17 Value)**
- Bookkeeping Basics Tutorial Video**($47 Value)**
- Video Reveals  How To Save Hundreds Of Dollars With A Tax Firm **($63 Value)**
- Updates When New Food Truck Strategies Are Discovered!**($200 Value)**